The Environmental Revolution

H.R.H. PRINCE PHILIP

The Environmental Revolution

Speeches on Conservation 1962-1977

ANDRE DEUTSCH

First published 1978 by
André Deutsch Limited
105 Great Russell Street London WC1

Copyright © 1978 by H.R.H. The Prince Philip
Duke of Edinburgh, KG, KT
All rights reserved

Printed in Great Britain by
W & J Mackay Ltd, Chatham

ISBN 0 233 97035 5

Contents

6 CONTENTS

Preface

It may seem unlikely but this book owes its origin to a camera I bought in Stockholm during the Equestrian Olympics of 1956. Later that year I attended the Summer Olympics in Melbourne, and it was on the long voyage home across the South Pacific, and a series of visits to British Antarctic Survey Bases and to the islands of the South Atlantic, that I began to use my newly acquired Hasselblad on the birds I saw from the Royal Yacht *Britannia*. This led to more bird-watching and to acquaintance with bird-watchers and naturalists, and so to the Council for Nature and the Wildfowl Trust. Almost before I could tell the difference between a Bewick and a Whooper, Peter Scott got me involved in the formation of the World Wildlife Fund and I found myself working with Aubrey Buxton and Max Nicholson in the organisation of the first of the 'Countryside in 1970' Conferences.

Looking back it is interesting to see how the gathering momentum of public interest generated by such people as Rachel Carson and Peter Scott swept the movement along from the Countryside Conferences to the European Conservation Year in 1970 and then to the climax at the great United Nations Conference on the Human Environment in Stockholm in 1972.

What started out as a movement for the conservation of nature and the natural environment soon acquired a new dimension – the conservation of the human environment. This in turn led to the Club of Rome and its famous publication in 1972, 'Limits to Growth', and also to the European Architectural Heritage Year in 1975.

In all this I suppose I could best be described as a 'front man'.

Consequently I found myself being asked to make an abnormally large number of speeches on a single group of subjects: the various aspects of conservation. The publishers have arranged the speeches by subject-matter rather than in strict chronological order, so that it is possible to dip into any particular subject at will, instead of reading the book from cover to cover. Inevitably I repeated the same points in more than one speech but any repetition has been avoided by taking extracts from the speeches, some of them quite short.

Now that the need for conservation is so generally appreciated, I hope it may interest people involved in various branches of conservation to read some of the arguments and views that were put forward at the time when the subject was first becoming a popular issue.

Foreword

The Environmental Revolution

Of all the remarkable shifts in popular interest since the war, nothing can quite compare with the sudden and explosive concern for the natural environment. It's a phenomenon that seems to have hit all the more industrially advanced countries at much the same time and at much the same speed. From a situation of almost total and apathetic indifference we are suddenly confronted by a massive and passionate concern for everything in and to do with nature and the pollution of the environment.

The conservation movement has meant a revolution in thought, and like all revolutions this one will probably go through much the same phases of development. To begin with the revolutionaries were dismissed as a lot of cranks and nutcases but as far as this revolution is concerned mounting evidence to support their case soon became obvious. The people who started it all were well aware of this evidence and many of them had spent quite some time thinking about what needed to be done, but as in all successful revolutions, the leaders have to face the danger of being swamped by the rank and file, whose enthusiasm is inclined to outrun their knowledge of the facts. Rational ideas are quickly ignored in the competitive rush to extremes.

This is probably the most dangerous phase because while it may be necessary to protest and revolt against indifference and neglect it is quite unnecessary to go to the opposite extreme by demanding a halt to all development or by seeking to pin the blame on any one particular group. Let's face it, we have all been indifferent in one way or another; finding a scapegoat achieves nothing, and emotion without the facts only makes enemies.

It would also be unfortunate if the environmental revolution fell into that other revolutionary trap – fragmentation. There are so many aspects of conservation that if every interest were to go its own way the whole movement would be disastrously weakened. Special interests and special cases there must be but their best chance of success lies in co-operation within one main body.

The next phase is the backlash: the counter-revolution, and this is always in direct proportion to the extremism of the original revolution. This backlash can appear in a number of different ways. The developers, the innovators or the exploiters – whatever you like to call them – are most unlikely to accept any restriction on opportunities without a fight. Then there is also the intellectual backlash. This takes the line that 'I'm bored to tears with all this talk of conservation, why don't all those hearty nature lovers go and get lost in the bush and leave us alone to enjoy our coffee and intelligent conversation in the comfort of the civilised city'.

A favourite argument is to suggest that all this concern about the environment is being generated by a lot of well-off people who merely want to make life better for themselves. The truth of course is that a poor environment affects the less well-off much more directly. It is the poor districts which suffer from pollution and lack of amenities; it is the crowded industrial urban areas which need space for recreation. The rich can escape from the noisy and dirty places, it is the poor who get stuck with them.

Then there are those who are in a position to do something about conservation, whether in government or industry, who may well be prepared to listen to reasonable arguments supported by accurate facts but who will certainly fight against threats and accusations, emotional outbursts and unpractical demands. Furthermore, if they are responding to public pressure rather than to personal conviction, they will be all the quicker to seize on to doubtful arguments.

Once the need for sensible conservation is recognised it becomes a matter of compromise. In exactly the same way that unrestrained material development and population increase will lead to disaster, so it is equally impossible and unrealistic to attempt a return to nature. We are committed to a technological way of life; the problem is to avoid destroying more of our natural environment than is absolutely necessary. If 'space-ship earth' is to continue to support life, mankind has got to learn to live in harmony and in balance with its resources.

A common feature of all revolutions is that no one bothers to keep the accounts; no one counts the cost. The bill for most revolutions is usually paid in human lives and the dead remain silent. In the environmental revolution the cost is in cash. Cash for sewage works, cash for anti-pollution equipment, cash for nature reserves and national parks, cash for water supplies and drainage, cash for research and many other things. The cost also shows in another way. Developments which are subject to pollution controls and conservation restrictions are more expensive than those which are not and this means that many of these restrictions need to be agreed between nations.

Revolutionaries have a way of overlooking these things. They are quick enough to accuse and demand but they are noticeably quiet or absent when someone passes the hat round to pay for the improvement. Conservation is like advice, it's always good for the other bloke.

The last phase of revolution is the return to apathy. This may be worse than the original apathy because people remember the revolution and assume that things have changed for keeps. In this respect conservation is like freedom. It can only be maintained by constant vigilance. Conservation is not something which we can do this year and then forget about. The natural human desire for profit is too strong to pass up an opportunity to exploit some resource or to increase productivity. It would be quite wrong and foolish to try and stop all development but it will need constant and careful attention to reconcile the desire for exploitation with the need for conservation.

I have suggested that the conservation movement has meant a revolution in thought. It means more than that, it means a revolution in administrative practice. Material and immediate prosperity is no longer the sole criterion for every development for whatever purpose.

A new criterion has been added, the conservation of the environment so that in the long run life, including human life, can continue. This new consideration must be taken into account at all levels and in all departments of government and in the boardrooms of every industrial enterprise. It is no longer sufficient simply to quantify the elements of existence as in old-fashioned material economics; conservation means taking notice of the quality of existence as well.

The problem is of course to give some value to that quality and perhaps the only way to do this is to try and work out the cost in terms of loss of amenities, loss of holiday and recreation facilities, loss of property values, loss of contact with nature, loss of health standards and loss of food resources, if proper conservation methods are not used. Looked at in that light it may well turn out that money spent on proper pollution control, urban and rural planning and the control of exploitation of wild stocks of plants or animals on land and in the sea, is the less expensive alternative in the long run.

The conservation of nature, the proper care for the human environment and a general concern for the long-term future of the whole of our planet are absolutely vital if future generations are to have a chance to enjoy their existence on this earth.

The Australian Conservation Foundation

CANBERRA, 24 APRIL 1970

PART ONE

The Natural Environment

The World Wildlife Fund

1962

The World Wildlife Fund may well be responsible for changing the course of world history. It has been formed in order to try and conserve the world's rapidly diminishing wildlife of all kinds. If it succeeds our descendants will have the pleasure of seeing wild animals. If it fails they will be forced to live in a world where the only living creature will be man himself, and his domestic animals. Always assuming, of course, that we don't destroy ourselves as well in the meantime.

Since the time of our Lord, that is in 1,962 years, about a hundred animals and the same number of birds have become extinct. Species that took at least 2½ million years to develop – wiped out for ever. The passenger pigeon which used to darken the skies of North America was exterminated – not as a pest but just for fun – in one human generation within the last hundred years. Today 250 species of animals and birds are in danger of extermination by the sheer callousness of mankind.

There are five reasons why animals are threatened all over the world.

First, physical conditions are changing; human population is increasing, forcing the animals out. Industry and science are polluting the air, the soil and the water, unintentionally maybe but none the less effectively killing off vast numbers of animals and fish.

Second, the means of controlling those creatures which are considered to be pests and nuisances are very much more powerful than ever before in history. They are in fact no longer means of control, they are methods of extermination. Even then things might not be so bad if they only affected the so-called pests; the trouble is that they set up a chain reaction in nature which takes in many innocent creatures and in some cases man himself.

Third, there are the killers for profit, the poachers, the get-rich-quick-at-any-cost mob. In Africa and elsewhere these thoughtless exploiters are slaughtering vast numbers of elephants merely because they can get 50 cents a pound for their ivory from a middleman who sells it to a receiver for double that. He in turn gets $2 a pound from an illegal dealer who charges the customer $5 a pound – the official price. Six hundred elephants a year are being killed merely because the game laws cannot be enforced and people want chessmen or a new set of billiard balls.

Fourth, the status-killers. In the Lebanon the *Times* correspondent reports that there is no longer a dawn chorus of birds because young men with shot-guns and air-guns prowl round the olive groves every morning and evening shooting everything that moves. You may well ask Why? – merely so that they can swagger back to the cities with tiny sparrow-sized birds dangling from their belts. Supposedly symbols of achievement – in fact they are badges of barbarity.

These status-killers are at work all over the world. Who hasn't heard the man boasting in the office or the club about his latest hunting or fishing success – not because he gets any pleasure out of it but merely because he thinks it is the thing to do.

You may condemn killing for sport but at least the true sportsman is concerned that the source of his sport is not destroyed; and you will find all true sportsmen willing and eager to co-operate with naturalists and conservationists whereas the status-killer couldn't care less. The fact is that like all imitators they impress no one and merely advertise a rather pathetic immaturity.

Finally, and probably most important, are the inadequate game and conservation laws and the means of enforcing them. Social justice may appear to demand the equal and unlimited right to kill animals but it does not seem much like natural justice if it results in the extermination of species. Conservation may mean complete protection but not necessarily. In most cases it means proper control. The mistake so often made by the ill-informed and the sentimental is that they are quite unable to see the difference between controlled conservation and indiscriminate destruction.

In Africa, for instance, there would be no need to impose complete protection on a great many animals. In fact if properly managed they could provide a very welcome protein addition to the people's diet. Many of the plains animals are as it happens far more thrifty and better suited to the conditions than any European livestock. What is more, thousands of people from all over the world will travel to see the great herds in their natural surroundings. These animals are in fact a vital economic asset to these countries so long as they continue to exist.

For conservation to be successful it is necessary to take into consideration that it is a characteristic of man that he can only be relied upon to do anything consistently which is in his own interest. He may have occasional fits of conscience and moral rectitude but otherwise his actions are governed by self-interest. It follows then that whatever the moral reasons for conservation it will only be achieved by the inducement of profit or pleasure.

The moral reasons for conservation must be obvious. After all we quite rightly collect vast sums of money and go to endless trouble to preserve man-made treasures most of which serve no practical purpose – surely then we should also pay some attention to the living God-made treasures of this world which have a practical as well as an aesthetic value.

Noah was commanded to build an ark and to take into it a pair of every living creature to save them from the flood. Today a different kind of deluge threatens the earth's creatures and the World Wildlife Fund is the ark built by men and women and children throughout the world to give them a chance to survive the thoughtless actions of mankind.

The problem the Fund is trying to tackle is enormous. It involves educating people, influencing governments, enforcing laws, initiating ecological and biological research, conducting surveys and sometimes buying land, or propagating threatened animal species in captivity rather like Noah.

Even so the Fund cannot hope to succeed on its own. What is

needed above all are people all over the world who understand the problem and really care about it. People with courage to see that the letter and the spirit of the conservation and game laws are obeyed and, where necessary, improved. People who care enough to bring up their children to have a proper respect and appreciation for wild animals.

Not just a few people here and there but literally hundreds of thousands of ordinary people, as well as naturalists and sportsmen, gamewardens and zoologists, so that we shall be able to say with satisfaction that at least in this one endeavour mankind was able to correct its mistakes in time by a conscious and deliberate effort of will and generosity.

World Wildlife Fund Dinner
NEW YORK, 7 JUNE 1962

The basic and most urgent purpose of the World Wildlife Fund is to help those species of animal which face extinction. It is not setting out to protect all animals from everything. It has no intention of campaigning against mouse-traps and fly-paper. Its function is to see that no other animal species goes the way of the dodo. Because the dodo, as you probably know, is a perfect example of the species of animal which has been totally exterminated. There is no living dodo left. And there never will be another one. I'm quite certain that stuffed dodos and even partly burnt ones which I think are the only ones left, or dodo skeletons, may be absolutely fascinating to some people. But I can't really believe that they compare with the live article.

I freely confess that a few years ago I had no idea whatever that all sorts of wild animal species were dying out. I had no idea, for instance, that since 1900 man has exterminated on an average one species every year. I'd even less idea that unless something pretty drastic was done fairly quickly, another thousand species of vertebrate animals might become extinct within the next few years. But even knowing all this didn't make any difference, until I began to find out why so many species – not individual animals, why so many species – are under sentence of extinction.

Broadly speaking, mankind is bringing about the extermination of animal species in three ways. First, by destroying the natural habitats of animals; and at this moment four of the most remarkable animals of the South American Andes are threatened with extinction, due to the destruction of the forest where they live. In Europe the numbers of the Spanish Imperial eagle, which is the largest and most handsome eagle in Europe, have been reduced by half in the last five years, because of the reduction of its living space. And this is the direct result of encroachment. Many of the effects are indirect.

The second way in which species become extinct is through indiscriminate commercial exploitation. A typical example of this is the whaling industry, which cleaned out the northern seas a hundred years ago, and is now in a fair way of reducing the whale population in the southern oceans. The blue whale, the largest animal in the world, and so far as is known, the largest animal there ever has been in the world, seems now to be on the very edge of extinction. Why? Because they produce, unfortunately for them, edible oils, cattle food, fertiliser, and the oil that makes your wrist watches go. Someone has estimated that in Australia sixty tons of kangaroo meat are processed every week, and a lot of it for pet food. This means that something like ten thousand kangaroos which includes all the little ones in the pouches are being killed weekly. This can't go on much longer before some of the rarer kinds are exterminated.

Even where controls have been imposed, it is not always possible to enforce them. For instance, despite every effort to protect them, the rhinoceros are being killed in very large numbers by poachers, who want their horns faster than the rhinos can grow them.

The third way in which we are reducing the wild animal population of the world is by indiscriminate fishing and shooting for sport. This has already caused the extinction of several species and put many more in danger. Protection and control came too late to save the passenger pigeon, and perhaps only just in time for the buffalo and the Eskimo curlew in North America. We are rather luckier in this country, because we've only got one wholly indigenous animal and that's the grouse. And that's got too many protectors. The ridiculous part about all this is that we have learned enough sense not to wipe out our domestic and farm animals, and sensible sportsmen take very good care not to wipe out game birds, mammals, or fish. In fact, naturalists and responsible sportsmen have come to recognise that they are allies in this matter of conservation.

Conservation means a combination of protection and control. For instance, the Royal Society for the Protection of Birds was mainly responsible for making it possible for the avocet to return to this country to nest. In order to achieve this, it has had to impose very strict controls on crows, rats, and certain gulls. I suppose it's conceivable that the question might be asked, Why should we try and save these animals from extinction? I thought about an answer to this long and often, and all I can say is that anyone who is capable of asking that question would be quite incapable of understanding the answer. The extermination of a species of animal is like the destruction of a unique work of art. Just imagine a group of vandals going around the world every year, and solemnly taking down all the work of one or two or two or three of the great masters and carefully and deliberately destroying them.

This Fund wants to bring home the facts about the threatened animals to as many people as possible, in order to gain their support. It wants to see that reasonable controls are placed upon those who cannot exercise self-control, and that these controls are properly enforced; and it wants to help all those people in agencies throughout the world who are taking active and practical steps to encourage conservation of rare species. To the majority of the people of this world – to them nature goes on, whatever they do. They struggle against the climate, against the pests that get at their gardens and farms, and therefore they find it hard to believe that mankind is actually changing the natural order of things. In fact this is just what is happening.

If we take action now, we can, indeed we must, prevent some of the worst tragedies mankind is committing in its thoughtless progress.

World Wildlife Fund: British National Appeal Banquet
LONDON, 6 NOVEMBER 1962

1969

In this age of confusion when we are all expected to be madly modern and frantically technological, the idea that anything needs to be conserved seems wildly improbable. All the real problems are concerned with the brave new world of machines and gadgets, houses and roads, so why suddenly all this fuss about wild animals? Most of them are nothing more than a nuisance anyway, some are pests and others cause diseases. Farmers don't like them, birds get in the way of aeroplanes, deer damage trees, foxes are eating inoffensive domestic cats, neighbourhoods are terrorised by mysterious panthers, and goodness knows what else.

Why then be concerned about the conservation of wildlife when for all practical purposes we would be much better off if humans and their domestic animals and pets were the only living creatures on the face of the earth? There is no obvious and demolishing answer to this rather doubtful logic although in practice the destruction of all wild animals would certainly bring devastating changes to our existence on this planet as we know it today.

The trouble is that everything in nature is completely inter-dependent. Tinker with one part of it and the repercussions ripple out in all directions. The extermination of a species in one part of the world can have just as serious consequences as the introduction of alien species, like the introduction of the rabbit in Australia.

Wildlife – and that includes everything from microbes to blue whales and from a fungus to a redwood tree – has been so much part of life on the earth that we are inclined to take its continued existence for granted.

Yet the wildlife of the world is disappearing, not because of a malicious and deliberate policy of slaughter and extermination, but simply because of a general and widespread ignorance and neglect.

In some cases, of course, near-extermination was brought about by commercial exploitation. In other cases where there is direct competition for land use between humans and wild animals, the animals inevitably lose, but I doubt whether the developers have ever thought of themselves as exterminators of wildlife.

Wildlife is not even safe from the quite indirect effects of industrialisation. Pollution of land and water and the inconsiderate use of chemicals play havoc with the natural environment of many animals and fish. I doubt whether industrial chemists and the producers of noxious effluents always appreciate the full importance of the part they play in the conservation or the destruction of nature.

It would be quite unfair to blame motorists for the number of birds and small animals, particularly hares, which they kill every year. Yet in some parts of Europe this is a significant factor in the survival of certain species.

In a few cases, a whole species has been wiped out for fun. However, this is more to do with the absence of proper control than any malicious intent. I don't imagine for one moment that the hunters individually or as a group actually set out to exterminate any particular type of bird. Anything which is free for all is liable to disappear pretty quickly.

If I may take it that you are broadly sympathetic to the idea that other forms of life have a valid right to continue to live on the earth and if I have convinced you that man either deliberately or unintentionally is responsible for the rapid disappearance of many forms of wildlife, then it only remains to suggest what needs to be done.

In the first place a much higher proportion of humans all over the world need to know and to understand the conservation issue.

Secondly, it should become a matter for international agreement and legislation that wild populations cannot be exploited without any sensible restrictions. It is perfectly reasonable to take a balanced crop but the breeding stock must be properly protected.

Thirdly, the problem of pollution in the air, in the land and in the water needs careful investigation and stringent control. This would benefit all living creatures, including ourselves and our domestic animals and pets.

Fourthly, most of the animal and plant populations, which are most severely threatened, need a more or less specialised environment. These special areas need to be recognised and given special protection. It's worth emphasizing here that it is not so much the plants and animals as individuals which need protection, it is the areas in which succeeding generations can live and mate and find their food that have to be protected from human take-over.

Fifthly, the whole world is now dominated by the works of man. This isn't an arrogant claim of human power – it's a simple practical fact. This places a special responsibility on us to maintain by deliberate action the balance between species and within environments which up till now has been maintained by nature. This means that some species must be given a great deal of artificial help; while other species need to be controlled and restricted. Conservation is not protection in the narrow sense. Conservation amounts to giving the other creatures a chance by maintaining the balance of nature – or perhaps a balance in nature – by design.

The conservation of nature may not strike the busy town-dweller as an enormously immediate or pressing problem but the people who know about these things – and we're not all cranks and crackpots – are only too well aware that if we don't take action now it may well be too late.

Malicious destruction is bad enough, but destruction by ignorance and neglect is unforgiveable.

World Wildlife Fund Dinner
YORK, 6 FEBRUARY 1969

1971

Ten years ago, the conservation of wildlife and the environment was a matter of no great concern and the voices raised in warning were like cries from the wilderness. Today, conservation in one form or another has become one of the most vital social and political issues of our age.

I suspect that the founders of the movement are astonished and delighted at what has happened in this time. To be strictly fair, this country had already achieved quite a lot in cleaning the air and the rivers before it became such a popular issue. Come to think of it, we haven't had a pea-soup fog in London for fifteen years, the hours of sunlight have increased, fish are coming back into the Thames, clogging power station inlets, and several plants and birds and insects are reappearing on open sites in the middle of cities.

Great strides have been made, but there is a tremendous lot still to be done. In spite of some spectacular achievements in the conservation of wildlife, I don't think that anyone would claim that the overall picture is better now than it was ten years ago. The human population continues to grow and the demands for everything it needs – water, land, resources – continue to grow with it. In many cases, the worst abuses of pollution have been checked but the flood of effluent continues to grow at an alarming rate. Exploitation of natural resources, which has created so many deserts in the past, is still a serious threat both to the land and its inhabitants as well as to the fish stocks of the seas and oceans. Anglers and fishermen would probably claim – and rightly – that things aren't what they used to be in the rivers and lakes.

Perhaps the main achievement of the last ten years is that now we do at least know what needs to be done, even if we cannot always agree at once how we should do it. We know the population needs to be stabilised; we know that parks and reserves are desperately necessary; we know that we must control the use of chemicals and effluent of all kinds; we know we must control the commercial exploitation of resources, particularly of wild animals, on land and in the oceans as well as forests and wetlands; and we know we must control sports, recreation and tourism. Every one of these requirements poses quite hideously difficult problems, but that is no reason to ignore them in the hope that they will go away. The problems will simply get bigger and more menacing till they menace human existence itself and destroy the only place we have to live. Economists can go on demanding growth, but even economists have yet to find a way of making our planet achieve a significant rate of growth.

In the end, conservation can only be achieved by voluntary subscription, by international government action, and it is my firm opinion that the World Wildlife Fund represents one of the most important and significant popular movements for the future welfare of mankind at work in the world today.

World Wildlife Fund Tenth Anniversary Dinner
LONDON, 4 NOVEMBER 1971

1977

Some years ago, when the first National Appeals for the World Wildlife Fund were being set up, I had a splendid, and what I hoped was a fairly original, line of patter about the fearful dangers facing the natural environment; about the unrestricted commercial exploitation of wild populations – the destruction of forests and wilderness areas to make room for the human population at the expense of their wild inhabitants – the pollution of land, rivers and oceans by both the deliberate as well as the unintentional spread of chemicals and effluents. But there is hardly any point in going into all that because I can only assume that it is your awareness of all these factors which has brought you here this evening. It seems to me that I have been asked to speak to the converted.

Converts are notoriously enthusiastic. So much so that their enthusiasm can sometimes overrun their understanding. I admit it is very confusing. For instance, if you have laboured to convince people that the population of Cape Barren geese is in danger, you shouldn't be surprised if the converts complain when a few years later permission is given to shoot them. If you have finally got the message home that we must be more considerate about wildlife, you look pretty silly when you appear to condone the culling of seals or the control of kangaroo populations. The trouble is that it is not easy to appreciate the difference between conservation and preservation. In other words, between maintaining a viable population within the resources of the available habitat on the one hand, and the absolute prohibition of any sort of interference on the other. On top of that it is not always easy to differentiate between genus and species.

I suspect the trouble begins when the assumption is made that the preservation of an endangered species means the same thing as the preservation of individual lives. In a desperate situation obviously every life counts, but it is quite possible to find a situation where a species is threatened by over-population and therefore liable to destroy its own habitat. It is in these cases that conservation includes population control. In some parts of the world it looks as if the human species – Homo sapiens – is destroying its own habitat by over-population without being able to appreciate the consequences.

Some wild populations, once their habitat is made secure, can be left to regulate themselves. Most bird populations come under this category, except, of course, those birds which have decided to share certain agricultural crops with the farmers. Other wild populations, notably fish and whales, have a commercial and nutritional value to man. Some people might like to see them preserved from any form of exploitation but, from the conservation point of view, all that is needed is to ensure that a viable population continues to exist. It is theoretically quite possible to establish a maximum sustainable yield for such populations which will not endanger the species as a whole. This has been tried by the International Whaling Commission, but if certain governments simply ignore the rules it is virtually impossible to do anything about it – short of sinking their whale catchers and factory ships.

The first consideration from the conservation point of view

is the survival of the species. I think it is also worth bearing in mind that the existence of far more species is threatened by the destruction of their habitats for all sorts of human socially and economically desirable reasons, than by direct capture and killing.

One last point: the natural environment is international. Many ground animals, a large proportion of birds and all the creatures of the seas are not limited in their movements by national boundaries. Furthermore, the problems of conservation in particular countries are not proportional to the ability or to the will to solve them. For example, in cases of migration the threats to a whole migratory route may be concentrated in one limited area. In other words, one country may be required to take measures quite out of proportion to its resources and which primarily benefit many others anyway. So the conservation of nature needs to be an international project, and it can only succeed by international co-operation. There is so much that needs to be done, but it can only be done with world-wide support and generosity.

World Wildlife Fund Dinner
WELLINGTON, NEW ZEALAND, 26 FEBRUARY 1977

The Canary in the Coalmine:
Wildlife Conservation

1967

It is becoming painfully obvious that unless the major land-users – that is, agriculturalists of all kinds, farmers, land reclamation officers, irrigation commissions, foresters, mineral developers, water and power engineers, city and highway planners – until these can be convinced of the need for a sensible conservation policy, the work and ambitions of the most energetic conservation societies will be brought to nothing.

The fact is that for the first time in history man has got complete control over his habitat. We can, if we so wish, or if we just let things slide, grossly over-populate the earth. We can, if we so wish, pollute the land, the water and the air. We can, if we so wish, exterminate any or all animals which might get in the way of our farms or cities. We can, if we so wish, convert all the jungles and the deserts and the swamps and the mountains into some form of usefully productive land. I daresay we could grow strawberries on the top of Mount Everest if we really tried. We can, if we so wish, cover the whole landscape with concrete to give all the motor cars a chance to drive about at the same time. If we can do all these things, surely we can decide what sort of habitat we would like to live in first and then make plans and arrangements to achieve it.

I don't aspire to speak for anyone else but I know what sort of habitat I would like to see. First I would like to see a stabilised world population so that we need make no further demands on land resources. I would like to see farming techniques in all countries developed in sympathy with the needs of wild populations, but to the point where no one need go hungry. I would like to see all land users show reasonable concern for the consequences of their plans so that mankind's needs for food, power, water, highways and cities can be met without unnecessary or avoidable destruction or dislocation of wild populations and the balance between them.

We have the power to do all these things now but we cannot do them until more people come to understand what is happening to the world's wildlife and come to see the vision of what the world could be like, and until there exists a general will and determination to achieve it.

It is not reasonable to expect hardworking farmers or hard-pressed engineers to visualise their activities as part of the broad sweep of human existence automatically. Life is too short, the day-to-day demands and problems are too immediate and the short-term aims of greater productivity, greater profit and more land under cultivation are more obvious. But this does not mean that they will reject the case for conservation out of hand. They are sensible and intelligent people and they will respond to sensible and intelligent argument. It is up to the conservation societies to make the approaches and to put forward their case moderately but with force and conviction.

There are many problems and situations which afflict the world over and over again. There will always be poverty and oppression. There always has been and there always will be. These are recurring problems requiring continuing solutions.

Conservation is dramatically different. It is really a case of now or never. Wildlife, whether in the shape of birds, animals, fish or plants, is being threatened and eroded as never before in history. If we don't get the answer right now, there won't be a second chance and this, our generation, will go down in history as the people who failed by neglect and indifference to take decisive control of our environment for the benefit of our successors in the future.

Canadian Audubon Society Dinner
TORONTO, 8 NOVEMBER 1967

1973

Years ago, it was the custom of miners to take a caged canary down the mine. It was not to listen to it singing, but simply to warn them in case the air began to get foul. If the bird looked a bit pale and sick, it was time to watch out. If it fell off its perch, it was time to get out.

I mention this because it so happens that it was the reduction in numbers, and in some cases the total disappearance, of species of animals which first alerted the world to the dangers of uncontrolled human expansion and development. What started out as a concern for the wild animals and wild places very soon became a concern about the effects of development on the human environment.

There is plenty of evidence that wildlife is being threatened and, in broad terms, this threat is due to the rapidly increasing human population, with its consequent demands for more living space, more agricultural land, more industry and transport facilities, more resources and to the consequent pollution of the land, air and water which these have been causing.

The solution to the problem of the natural environment is not very difficult in principle, but it has some quite serious snags in practice. Setting aside wilderness areas, in which the wild animals can live, is the obvious answer. The trouble is that it is just those areas which are wanted for new agricultural land, for housing, for mineral and timber resources, for water storage and all sorts of other purposes. In addition, many of the areas are either already partly inhabited, or at least used in some parts of the world, by nomadic peoples.

There are, of course, many wild populations, particularly wild birds, which have existed together with human populations from time immemorial. Their problems are rather different and, in many cases, things like pesticides, herbicides, drainage schemes and changes in the pattern of farming have either removed their food supply or their nesting possibilities. There is a further difficult problem, well known in Australia and New Zealand, and that is the effect of introduced wild or domestic species, which have gone wild, upon the indigenous populations. The rabbit, the buffalo and the camel are the most obvious examples.

The threat to the natural environment very quickly alerted people to the threat to their own, the human environment. After all, if fish and birds are being poisoned by polluted waters, it will be our turn next. If wild places are being threatened by increasing human population, what about places for human recreation? If the animals are running out of food, perhaps it is about time to worry about food supplies for the growing number of people. Furthermore, higher standards of living for more people are going to demand even more resources. Are they sufficient? While everything else can grow, we know that the earth is finite and the sort of resources we are using today also have an ultimate limit. We read gloomy prophecies of almost immediate doom, written by reputable scientists working in highly respected institutions. We also read categoric denials and refutations by equally respectable scientists. Both sides accuse the other of lack of realism, fudging the figures and omitting considerations which do not suit their theories.

I can only say that I do not find the evidence for almost immediate doom convincing. I accept the dangers of an ever increasing human population and I recognise the damaging effects of pollution. I am not at all convinced about the inevitable exhaustion of all useable resources within the foreseeable future.

While I do not think doom is inevitable or immediate, I am ever more convinced that doom is much more likely if we try to de-develop or turn against technology and science as the causes of our difficulties. I can think of nothing more foolish than to pick on them as scapegoats when what we should be doing is to use them to get us out of our difficulites. We will not be able to control pollution or land erosion without the help of technology. We will not be able to solve our water supply problems, our energy needs, or the problems of resource substitution without massive scientific research. The essential need is to point their energies and activities in the right direction.

The help of technology and science is equally important in the conservation of nature. This is not a simple matter of blanket preservation. We must know precisely what areas and conditions are significant to the survival of species. This cannot be decided by emotional response; we must have the facts. Just as there is no point in trying to control, at great expense, a form of pollution which does no material harm, equally there is no reason to prevent all forms of resource exploitation and any further industrial development.

Concern for nature is an emotional issue and it is very important that people should feel strongly about it but, at the same time, the action which follows must be strictly rational. If you see a fire starting in your house, you hardly need a computer to tell you that if you do nothing about it your house will burn down. The point is to start putting the fire out before it spreads.

Parliamentary Luncheon
CANBERRA, 14 MARCH 1973

Over the past several years the change in general attitudes to animals, wildlife and the natural and human environment has been quite dramatic. In the first place, most of the specialist bodies concerned with the study of conservation of particular species, or groups of animals or plants, or geographical areas, all started to notice independently that things were beginning to go wrong at about the same time – roughly during the 1950s. The outcome was the foundation of the World Wildlife Fund followed by the first 'Countryside in 1970' Conference, which fully confirmed their suspicions that the countryside in this country and wildlife all over the world were facing serious trouble.

It is becoming quite apparent that a very large number of animals and plants simply cannot co-exist with human occupation of land. They are not compatible with intensive cultivation, dense urbanisation or industrialisation. In some cases overlapping is possible, particularly in water and in the air. The problem, therefore, of conservation is that the direct protection of individual species is not really effective except under zoo conditions. If wildlife is to continue, whole areas will need to be set aside and the wild population contained and managed within them in such a way that people can see the animals without disturbing their natural existence more than absolutely necessary. The great African parks show that this can be done very effectively.

If this is an accceptable theory, it raises the rather interesting idea that zoological gardens and collections are beginning to come closer to conservation areas. Both depend on the principle of the direct management of wildlife. The only major difference is that zoos collect from all over the world, whereas conservation areas are concerned with the protection of indigenous species.

There are, of course, certain special considerations which will have to be taken into account in the management of wildlife protected areas. Migration is an obvious example, and wild populations which are used as a source of food or for commercial or sporting purposes will also need very particular treatment.

The concept that all wildlife will have to be specially managed in order to allow it to survive at all raises some other rather interesting ideas.

Human mobility has become such that it might be asked whether, in the long run, it would not be better for all concerned if people were to go where the animals are at home rather than trying to bring the animals to where the people are at home. In any case, as the pressure on wild species continues to increase, the need for special collections will be greater than it is today. In addition, the whole business of scientific study through comparative physiology and comparative medicine will become more important, while the skills and techniques of animal management in zoos will become increasingly valuable to the management of conservation areas.

Annual General Meeting, The Zoological Society
LONDON, 23 MAY 1973

Traditionally the interest in natural history and in wild animals comes in two forms. There are the realists who feel that nature is either a threat to their livelihood or a resource to be exploited. The other attitude is rather more romantic; it maintains that nature is to be admired and therefore preserved. For generations these two attitudes existed in uneasy balance, but then a third factor entered the situation. Activities which had nothing to do with the exploitation or the protection of nature began to make their presence felt. These activities were of two separate but related kinds.

In the first place the human population had begun to increase very rapidly. The consequent spread of housing, the transport systems, the growing demand for water and food, and the mounting flood of effluent and waste products, started to put tremendous pressure on the open country, and particularly on so far undeveloped country. Secondly, the enormous growth of industrial activity with its own increasing demand for power for mineral resources and for land and water, and with its own problem of waste and effluent disposal, added to the pressure on the natural environment.

At the same time the exploiters of nature, farmers, foresters, fishermen, fur trappers and all the rest, began to improve their methods with the help of better chemistry, better botany, better biology and better technology. This combined onslaught was really too much for those who felt that wild populations of animals and plants had a reasonable right to continue to co-exist with man on this limited planet.

Rachel Carson sounded a dramatic warning in her book, *Silent Spring*, while the leaders of the movement for the conservation of nature, such as Sir Peter Scott, set to work to mobilise international opinion. They formed the World Wildlife Fund, they strengthened the International Union for the Conservation of Nature and Natural Resources, and many countries, not previously very concerned about these matters, set up their own protection and preservation societies, and eventually the whole issue was taken up at a popular and then at a political level.

To begin with there was a period of confrontation. The exploiters of wild populations were particularly upset because they thought that their livelihood was being threatened, and anyway they maintained that their operations were traditional and no serious harm had been done so far. However, history can show plenty of cases to prove that this sort of exploitation only ceases either with the extermination of the wild population concerned or with the introduction of rational controls which are the basis of all good husbandry.

The cod war is a part of this confrontation process. There is also the salmon war and the whale war and the capture-of-rare-wild-animals-for-safari-parks-and-zoos war and the shooting-of-rare-wild-animals-for-the-collection-of-trophies war. All these activities can continue but not under the present uncontrolled conditions which will inevitably lead to the extinction of a number of species.

Certainly our human existence is very important; naturally we don't want people to starve or to be out of work or to lack homes and education, health and recreation, but surely not at any cost, and surely not at the cost of so many things which can make life on this earth so fascinating and rewarding?

In this sense conservation of nature is partly a practical and partly a moral issue. There is no absolute right and wrong about it, it is simply what individual people believe to be right and wrong, and the sort of world they would like to live in. For all practical purposes we could survive in a concrete jungle living on some nutrient material. I have no doubt we could cram a lot more people on to this globe if we did something like that, but do we really want to take the risk of making that sort of existence inescapable for the generations which will be coming after us? If we just shrug our shoulders and say, well, that is their problem, we must remember that it is this generation which will have condemned them to these conditions. Our decision will make their problem.

There are certain things in this life which are common to all occupations and professions and one of them is the natural environment. Some people, by their work and activities, have more effect on it than others, but the earth is our home, it is what we all have to live in, and the quality of the natural environment, which we bequeath to the next generation, depends upon the attitude of every single one of us, whatever we do for a living and whatever we do with our leisure.

University of Salford Degree Ceremony (1)
SALFORD, 16 JULY 1973

Engineering in Agriculture

Mechanisation enters into every operation to do with the use of land for agriculture. Land reclamation, irrigation, drainage, cultivation, cropping, handling, storage and finally transport are all dependent upon engineering and mechanical equipment. In fact, apart from pesticides and fertilisers, the one single factor which has been responsible for increased agricultural productivity is mechanisation.

In those countries where mechanisation has been introduced, about 4 per cent of the population is capable of producing from 60 to more than 100 per cent of the national food requirements. In many other countries 70 per cent of the population engaged in cultivation cannot do as well. What would happen in India, for example, if the cultivators dropped to 4 per cent hardly bears thinking about, but that only means that mechanisation must be introduced in a way most suitable to Indian conditions.

In the case of India and other areas with similar problems, irrigation and drainage can bring more land into cultivation and the mechanisation of handling, storage and transport can make an important contribution. Only the mechanisation of cultivation and cropping would have to be tailored to the needs of small farmers. This is as much a social, economic problem as the simple mechanisation of agriculture.

The very powers of engineering cause their own problems. For instance, land reclamation is eroding the wild areas of the world which are the last refuges of our fellow creatures. We can well ask whether it is in man's long-term interest to wipe out the remaining wildlife. One can also well ask whether it is in man's long-term interest to go on increasing the world population.

There are two sides to the solution of the problem of malnutrition, more food or a stabilised population.

Then the very intensity of cultivation which mechanical devices make possible raises the problem of maintaining the soil fertility.

Water is another problem. Human civilisation is demanding more and more fresh water and agriculture has one of the most urgent claims on the available supplies. Draining swamps, diverting rivers, creating reservoirs and all the other things which engineers do with water, are changing our whole environment.

There are really two sides to engineering as it affects agriculture. There are first those structures, techniques and machines which are directly used by producers. By that I mean the machinery and installations which individual farmers acquire and control themselves. This in itself is a rapidly expanding area. If combine harvesters immediately spring to mind, they are only the thin end of the wedge. Virtually every type of soil has its specialised cultivators, virtually every crop has its specialised harvester; every process for the application of fertilisers, weed and pest controls have their own machines from aircraft to knapsack tanks. Milking arrangements, the preparation and distribution of fodder and the collection of manure are all in the process of mechanisation, if not automation.

The other side is perhaps even more important. It might be called the infra-structure of agriculture. This includes everything from a regional reclamation and irrigation system, such as the Gezira Cotton Scheme in the Sudan, for instance, to the equipment and installations required to collect, process and store agricultural produce. Not least important is the transport network and specialised transport equipment which alone can decide whether remote areas can become profitable producers.

Another important part of this infra-structure is the invention and development of new machines and installations. Much of this is done by the manufacturers but there is also a need for research establishments looking even further ahead. Needless to say nothing can happen without a strong corps of suitably trained technologists and technicians, conversant with the farmers' practical problems and requirements.

We all know only too well that city people have always maintained a rather patronising air of superiority over the bumbling and old-fashioned farmer. I am not going to suggest that city people are totally lacking in intelligence so I can only assume that this superiority is due to simple ignorance. The fact of the matter is that farmers in the technologically advanced countries have progressed just as fast as any other industry. In fact, any comparison in the increase of their productivity with other industries shows that they have done far better than average. Indeed, in some cases productivity has grown faster than the city gentlemen planned for, with the anomalous result that in some areas there was too much food in a world suffering from a chronic shortage.

All this has come about through the active co-operation and understanding between farmers, scientists and engineers. Between them they have shown that they can transform agriculture and it is quite apparent that the possibilities for the future are even greater. I believe it is only by attempting to become aware of these possibilities that we can ensure that the changes which engineering is bringing about are not only profitable, but, as far as we can tell, are in the long-term interests of mankind.

Royal Agricultural Society of the Commonwealth Conference
TORONTO, 8 NOVEMBER 1967

Research into Forestry

People might well be forgiven for wondering why there should be any need for research into forestry. Trees are so much a part of the background of our existence, they seem so natural and permanent that it may be difficult to realise that they constitute any problem. Yet the fact is that people have been destroying the world's forests for thousands of years. Many of the most arid deserts are the result of forest destruction and the subsequent over cropping and over grazing.

Forests are usually remote from centres of population and even where they occur in the vicinity of cities, the fact that they are being properly cropped and managed is not immediately obvious to the casual passer-by. Neither is it at all self-evident that forests constitute one of the world's largest sources of renewable raw materials.

As many communities have discovered to their cost, even the richest mineral deposits eventually run out and all that is left is a vast hole in the ground. With care and forethought the supply of timber, with the increasing range of timber products and cellulose, can go on for ever.

The odd thing is that we seem to be at a sort of halfway stage in our attitude to resources. In agriculture or in the extraction of minerals we have long since discovered that a free-for-all exploitation is quite impossible. Cultivation and stock rearing is now a continuing process of cropping and reproduction and mineral extraction is by organised concession.

On the other hand sea fishing, and various other wild populations, and, in many places, forests are exploited as if they were an inexhaustible bounty provided by a benevolent God for a people determined not to know the facts.

Forests are important natural resources which we simply cannot afford to go on exploiting indiscriminately. Furthermore they also constitute the last remaining wild areas free from the constant interference of man and therefore the last refuge of many wild populations.

It is only too easy to argue that most wild animals and plants are not only useless to man but in many cases active pests and nuisances. So why bother about them? There is no practical or rational answer. Either you have grown up with a consideration for your natural surroundings and sympathy for your fellow creatures or you have not. Either you believe in the continuing pattern of existence on this earth or you believe that everything must be subordinate to the material interests of men. Either you believe that man now wields the ultimate power over the destiny of the earth and all its creatures and therefore that we have a moral responsibility to exercise that power with restraint and consideration; or you believe that what we call 'nature' can look after itself.

There is one aspect of forests which is directly useful to man, but not in the commercial sense. With a human population explosion on our hands and the increasing pressure on land area for habitation and cultivation, only the forests will be left as major areas for recreation and refreshment.

Research into forestry is therefore a vitally important activity. It is essential if we are to conserve, develop and manage important yet dwindling raw material. It is a determining factor in the reclamation of man-made deserts. It can help to find new uses for timber products. It can advance the whole concept of trees as a direct food source for various kinds of stock, and as I have suggested, it can make an immensely valuable contribution to the whole problem of the conservation of wild populations both plant and animal.

Opening of Forestry Building, Australian National University
CANBERRA, 16 MAY 1968

Pollution: The Deadly Cloud

The industrial followed by the scientific revolution, combined with a world population explosion, have produced one of the most serious situations that the world has experienced since the flood. The sheer weight of numbers of the human population, our habitations, our machinery and our ruthless exploitation of the living and organic resources of the earth; together these are changing our whole environment. This is what we call progress and much of this development is naturally to the direct and welcome benefit of mankind. However, we cannot at the same time ignore the awkward consequences and the most direct and menacing, but not the only consequence of this change, is pollution.

Pollution is a direct outcome of man's ruthless exploitation of the earth's resources. Experience shows that the growth of successful organic populations is eventually balanced by the destruction of its own habitat. The vast man-made deserts show that the human population started this process long ago. There are two important differences today. In the first place the process has gone from a walking pace to a breakneck gallop. Secondly we know exactly what is happening. If not exactly in all cases, we know enough to appreciate what is happening and the need to take care.

There have been isolated areas of pollution ever since the first coal mines washed coal dust into the rivers and the first metal smelting works gushed every kind of toxic waste into the air and into the water. You have only to look at the derelict land in the South Wales valleys to see the destruction caused by those operations. These were prophetic demonstrations of the danger of pollution but they were local and they were accepted in the interests of progress and employment. No one recognised them as awful warnings of what was to follow. Today pollution has reached a level of intensity which very few even dreamed about as little as twenty years ago.

Let me briefly outline the main causes. First, industrial pollution: this can take the form of atmospheric effluents which damage or destroy living organisms, reduce visibility and solar radiation or, through the interaction of rain, pour down various toxic or destructive chemicals on land and sea. Manufacturing industries are also enormous consumers of fresh water and in many cases the water-borne effluents can be extremely destructive. Even when the water is treated and returned as clean it certainly does not have the same characteristics as the raw water had before it was used.

Then there are various forms of pollution caused by the production of energy from both thermal and nuclear power stations, motor vehicles, trains, aircraft, ships and the rest. Nuclear waste products are a problem in themselves but all these sources are responsible for growing atmospheric pollution. On top of that the power stations are immense consumers of cooling water and the effect of this is to raise the temperature of the water of the rivers, estuaries and coastal sea water to an extent which sharply affects the whole biological structure in the area.

Then again pollution is caused by the application of various chemicals directly to the land in the form of pesticides, fungicides, insecticides and the rest. In this I include the extremely dangerous habit of throwing away containers of powerful chemicals which are not quite empty. The original intention may be very useful but the consequences affect everything which exists on the land, whether animal or vegetable. Furthermore, these things are then washed into the rivers and consequently they affect water supplies and the marine biology right down to and including the sea.

There is pollution by industrial products. This can vary from virtually indestructible plastics, whether sheets or containers, to all the derelict and no longer useable things such as old motor cars and bedsteads, in fact the whole vast and growing problem of domestic waste disposal.

Probably the most dangerous pollution is caused by pumping raw untreated sewage straight into rivers or into the sea. From time immemorial man has dumped all his waste products into the nearest river. With today's immense urban populations this has resulted in every major river in the world becoming nothing better than a convenient open sewer with all the consequent hazards to health and to all the other living creatures who also inhabit this earth.

This may give the impression that pollution only affects the sea and the fish in it. The point is of course that all forms of pollution end up in rivers, lakes and the sea. There are many other factors which are causing the destruction of wild populations of plants and animals just as effectively but pollution is one of the most effective.

Pollution is no longer a matter of local incidents, today it has the whole biosphere in its grip. The processes which devastated the Welsh valleys a hundred years ago are now at work, over, on and under the earth and the oceans. Even if we bury all this waste underground there still remains the risk that toxic materials through chemical reactions will be washed out and into underground water courses. If ever there was an area of research more closely related to human welfare it is the problem of the safe disposal of waste and effluents.

The fact is that we have got to make a choice between human prosperity on the one hand and the total well-being of the planet Earth on the other. Even then it is hardly a choice because if we only look for human prosperity we shall certainly destroy by pollution the earth and the human population which has existed on it for millions of years. We talk about over- or under-developed countries; I think a more exact division might be between the under-developed and over-populated. The more people there are, the more industry and the more waste and the more sewage there is, and therefore the more pollution.

At the moment it seems as if pollution is too remote for most people. Indeed, judging by the amount of rubbish of all kinds which the average citizen chucks out of his car or dumps on every available parking, camping or picnic site, he is unlikely to feel any concern for pollution on a grander scale. Every year on the public roads in certain parts of the country which I know personally the situation gets worse. Every parking place becomes a stinking dump of rotting rubbish. I see this myself every season and I can only assume that the same applies all over the country. What astonishes me is that so many people continue to ignore the possibility that anyone else might like to use the same site after them. This is not special pleading because I have no wish and no need to use these sites myself, but I do know that there are any number who will be using them. It is this general lack of concern for the future which worries me, particularly as precisely this situation exists on a global scale.

If the world pollution situation is not critical at the moment it is as certain as anything can be that the situation will become increasingly intolerable within a very short time. The situation can be controlled and even reversed but it demands co-operation on a scale and intensity beyond anything achieved so far.

I realise that there are any number of vital causes to be fought for, I sympathise with people who work up a passionate concern about the all too many examples of inhumanity, injustice, and unfairness, but behind all this hangs a really deadly cloud. Still largely unnoticed and unrecognised, the process of destroying our natural environment is gathering speed and momentum. If we fail to cope with this challenge, all the other problems will pale into insignificance.

Edinburgh University Union
EDINBURGH, 24 NOVEMBER 1969

European Conservation Year, 1970

1969

A few years ago anyone voicing any concern about conservation and environment was looked upon as a harmless sort of crank, to be humoured at best and denounced as alarmist at worst. Today, strange as it may seem, it has become almost decent to be concerned about the protection of wildlife, to worry about the destruction of the countryside, to feel anxiety about the indiscriminate use of chemicals in agriculture, and the use of antibiotic drugs in animal feeding stuffs, or to take an interest in water resources. It's no longer bad form to express horror at the worst excesses of pollution.

Not so long ago we were being told that a nation's wealth depended upon the number of its workers and the level of domestic consumption. Today there is a nagging suspicion that the population growth in this country from 50 to 70 million and the motor car growth from 10 to 28 million by the year 2000 is going to have its problems.

Twelve more cities the size of Birmingham and three times as many cars is a pretty daunting prospect. Finding employment is going to be difficult enough, making provision for leisure is only going to make a critical situation even more acute. Furthermore, the cost of the necessary social services and facilities will run up a colossal bill. Whichever way you look at it there are difficulties. For instance, it is rapidly becoming apparent that natural water supplies are no longer sufficient. Converting a large part of our land area into reservoirs and using our rivers as domestic drains is really the height of waste and folly.

We must face up to the absolute certainty that we shall have to use de-salted sea-water in the very near future. The only alternative that I can see is a series of urban islands surrounded by fresh-water lakes.

Multiply all these difficulties for Europe and the sheer size of the problem is enough to make even the most complacent pause for thought.

I think the simple truth is that everyone of reasonable intelligence has become aware of what is wrong with our environment. They have come to realise that our honeymoon period with science and technology is over. They have come to understand the immense and damaging pressures which have been put upon the countryside and all wild populations on land or in the water. We've now got to settle down and attempt to cope with the consequences. And as so often happens after honeymoons the consequences are unexpected.

In this case many of the solutions depend upon informed and intelligent compromise. We have two problems. The first is the need to correct the mistakes of the past, to put right the things which we now know to be wrong and dangerous. And the second problem is to make certain that we do not make any unnecessary or glaring mistakes for the future.

We are no longer concerned with the problem of opening people's eyes to what is happening. From now on the problem will be to create the right kind of administrative organisation to cope with the conservation of our environment. By that I don't mean the preservation of every tree and bush, or the halting of industrial development, and I don't mean an exclusive concern for our dumb friends. The conservation of our environment takes in much more. It includes refuse disposal, pollution, building, industrial development, transport, leisure activities, agriculture, wildlife, water resources, extraction, noise, unsightliness, smell and dirt. These things are all inter-related. They all have an influence on the quality of existence for all people and they cannot be dealt with piecemeal.

In most cases we know what is wrong and we are also quite capable of putting it right. However, in order to put things right the voluntary bodies must re-arrange and co-ordinate themselves so that they can mobilise public opinion in the right direction and offer their advice in concert. Equally important, the statutory bodies must come to recognise that this subject really matters for the long-term welfare of the people. Here and there some quite impressive results have been achieved, but if the authorities want to make any coherent impressions in the future they will need to adjust their administrative system accordingly. They must make themselves capable of effective action now and effective planning for the future. This means that legislation needs to be backed up by competent and cost-effective government management. Without it the seventy million inhabitants of this island in the year 2000 may well have no leisure and nothing to do with it, except perhaps to watch natural history programmes made for television in the sixties.

It is my hope that 1970, European Conservation Year, will go down in history as the year in which mankind stopped letting things happen and decided to take intelligent and effective control of his environment.

Dinner given by the Corporation of London to inaugurate European Conservation Year, 1970, in the U.K.
LONDON, 16 DECEMBER 1969

1970

Concern for our natural environment in Europe is nothing very new. Almost every country in Europe can point to a club or society founded any time up to three hundred years ago for the study or protection of animal and plant life. In most European countries zoological gardens and game parks have been in existence for even longer.

Europeans did not restrict their interest in conservation to their home countries. Colonial administrations had an excellent record in the protection of forests from exploitation and in the establishment of nature reserves to protect populations of wild animals. This policy has been successfully continued in most of the newly independent countries and in many cases it forms the basis of a prosperous tourist trade and a key factor in their economics.

It is also worth remembering that most of the world's flora and fauna was catalogued and classified by Europeans. I suspect that the rest of the world still looks upon the dedicated bird-watcher, or the collection of everything from acephalan molluscs to Zabrus beetles, as a form of madness peculiar to Europeans.

The problem facing us today is that there are some entirely new factors changing Europe's already artificial balance of nature. People realise that the last hundred years have witnessed a scientific and technological explosion. Most people are now aware that there has also been an increase in human population to almost plague proportions. What is less obvious perhaps is the penalty we have to pay for the enormous improvement in human material standards. The fall-out from the technological explosion has littered Europe with immense industrial complexes belching pollution into the air and into the water, while the increase in human population has created cities bigger than the world has ever known and intense overcrowding in almost all parts of the continent.

By a strange irony it is the growing urban populations, and not country people, who will be the first to feel any deterioration of the environment.

Between them technology and mankind have created a vast network of road, rail and air transport systems and a problem in refuse and waste disposal which has completely defeated our efforts to control it. Meanwhile increasing leisure has released millions of people into the mountains and on to the beaches. We failed to notice the effect all this was having on the environment and now we are facing a crisis situation. We have suddenly become aware that European land-locked seas and lakes are in greater danger of becoming deserts than the land. It is said of Lake Erie in the United States that it is so polluted that if any-one falls into it they don't drown, they just decay. This could happen here.

For generations agriculture has been a partnership with

nature; today the pressure to increase output is so intense that farmers have to grasp at every chemical and mechanical means of increasing production and they have to bring every available acre into use. Intensive rearch helps them to destroy the pests and weeds, but such destruction inevitably interferes with some long-established delicate food chain.

All over Europe there are formidable problems to be faced and overcome. In the first place we need to assess the legitimate demands for land for industrial and city development and for water storage. We need to strike a balance between the control of pests and the destruction of wildlife, bearing in mind that animals don't know much about frontiers between nations.

We must find a way to control the exploitation of wild fish stocks in the open oceans. We must decide whether our inland seas are to continue to sustain life or slowly become polluted rubbish dumps. We need to decide whether we want to use our rivers and lakes as a supply of domestic water, or for sport and recreation, or as carriers of re-cycled industrial water or to let them rot as sewers, they cannot be used for all these purposes. We have got to learn how to handle our own waste products and effluents.

In any case the natural supply of water will soon be unequal to the demand and we shall have to develop other sources of supply. We must decide how much pollution of the air, the land and the water we are prepared to tolerate. We must make a fair allocation of land and water for agricultural purposes and for different types of leisure occupations and recreations.

In order to make these decisions we need to create an administrative system which is capable of formulating a sensible and comprehensive conservation policy, which can take, preferably, the right decisions and which can eventually carry the policy and decisions into effect. It must distinguish between those aspects of conservation which can be dealt with by advice and encouragement and those which require legislative action. This is an immensely difficult process because conservation is to do with people. Every restriction, every control, and every development, inevitably makes a direct impact on the life of particular individuals or groups of people. I need hardly add that the system must make it possible to agree and enforce international controls where these are found to be necessary.

Above all we have got to face the unpalatable fact that the conservation of our environment is going to cost a very great deal of money, and the denser the human population becomes the more expensive it will be.

It is no longer a question of stimulating interest and concern, or of discussing present mistakes and future dangers. People are already showing signs of boredom with all this talk about conservation. Even without any further research we know enough to be able to put many things right.

The fact is we cannot postpone decisions any longer. The process of destruction of living things cannot be reversed. The burden of responsibility for the future of Europe rests squarely on us and our generation.

It is just as well to recognise that any measures taken to protect our environment will be unpopular in some quarters and they will inevitably cut across national boundaries. They will certainly be condemned as unwarranted interference or for preventing necessary development. Some will be politically inconvenient, others will be dismissed as administratively awkward. It will be extremely difficult but we must find ways to compromise between conservation and development.

The starving millions are always used as justification for any agricultural toxic chemical. The public interest in the short term can always justify yet another encroachment, yet another water storage scheme, yet another exploitation of national resources. This is inevitable and some objections may well be valid, but if we want to continue to live a reasonably civilised existence in an increasingly overcrowded world we shall have to accept certain restrictions and make special and expensive alternative arrangements.

The problem which confronts Europe and indeed the whole world, is to decide what restrictions are necessary to protect our natural environment from our own exploitation.

Time is fast running out and it remains to be seen whether

those in political authority can shoulder their responsibilities in time and act quickly enough to relieve a situation which grows more serious every day.

European Conservation Year 1970 Conference
STRASBOURG, 9 FEBRUARY 1970

Water is no Joke

I believe that 1973 will go down as the year in which the public, as a whole, became really aware that water is a serious problem. For years, indeed for generations, a clean and unlimited supply of water has been taken for granted. Any shortage was assumed to be due to mismanagement, and any limitation on supply was considered to be a plot against the ordinary citizen. It was too easy to make jokes about our rainfall. I believe we are seeing the end of that attitude. I believe that the general development of interest in conservation and the environment has made a great many people realise that water is no joke and that any further drastic increase in demand could well produce a serious crisis unless some quite radical developments take place.

For instance, there seems to be a surviving assumption that rivers can be both suppliers of clean water as well as collectors of effluent. A domestic or even a housing estate system based on that principle would be a disaster. In theory, what happens in the home should happen across the country. Once water has been abstracted, it should remain segregated from the natural supply in the rivers, and all treatment and re use should take place in a wholly independent system. Expensive, maybe, but then so is the domestic system if you compare it to the village pump and bucket system which went before it.

If the word conservation means anything at all in relation to the natural environment, it means that we should try to keep our rivers as near their natural state as possible. If anyone suggests that water which has been used for any purpose and treated, is the same as the natural water in the river, I am afraid he is talking nonsense.

Rivers which flow through towns and cities are naturally much more difficult to manage than those which run through open country, but we have got to get away from the idea that we can discharge anything we like into them or even into their estuaries.

Theoretically, the obvious point at which to abstract clean water is as near as possible to the mouth of a clean river. That is the point of maximum flow. After treatment and recycling through a piped system, the eventual treated effluent should not go back into a river or even into an estuary, but out to sea where the tidal effect can help the mixing and diluting process.

The time was when all reservoirs were sacrosanct and any form of recreational activity was very strictly forbidden. Things have got much better but the problem of the recreational use of water still hasn't been solved. The trouble is that you can't really sail and waterski, skin-dive and fish, bird-watch and powerboat race, scull and swim, protect and encourage breeding birds, and canoe, all on the same piece of water. Sooner or later there will have to be much more drastic segregation between the active and passive uses and zoning between the individual activities.

Of all the works of man, apart from his physical occupation of land in the form of urbanisation and industrialisation, the exploitation of water resources and the general management of water has the most direct and significant impact on the natural environment. Pollution is probably the worst offender, but it is controllable and it is being controlled. Damming and draining and all the works that go with them, on the other hand, can change the countryside quite drastically, but if they are done with consideration and with a proper understanding of the natural factors, their damaging effect can be substantially reduced.

However, I don't think conservationists will ever look very happily on proposals to drown more valleys or to see the last remaining pieces of wetland drained. I think it would be putting it mildly to say that they look with horror on the plans to build huge barrages in major river estuaries. Many of our traditional attitudes served very well in the past and they may well still be valid for the future, but circumstances have changed beyond measure and perhaps our solutions to the problems of the future may have to change with them.

Association of River Authorities Conference
LLANDUDNO, 16 MAY 1973

Fuel and the Environment

Fuel and the environment have been causing serious problems for mankind ever since the earliest times. Our difficulties are nothing new, they are just a bit more sophisticated. There are many parts of the world which at one time supported flourishing civilisations but which are now useless deserts or barely support goat-herding nomads at the lowest level of human existence. We know that those areas had great forests and rich agricultural land but we also know that, like all living organisms, human communities grow in numbers to consume the resources available.

The forests disappeared as they were exploited for fuel and building material while the fertility of the soil was destroyed by overgrazing and overcultivation. These ancient civilisations collapsed because they could not deal with their energy crisis and because they destroyed the natural environment upon which they depended. I daresay, of course, that they were also plagued by waste disposal problems, pollution, particularly of water supplies, soil erosion, urban renewal difficulties and, in the last resort, by wars.

Eventual equilibrium is maintained by the rate of regeneration balanced by the control on population numbers exerted by climate, availability of minimum levels of food and fuel, and by disease. In a mild climate human life can exist at a very much lower standard than in a harsh climate, which makes regeneration in some of those areas to a level high enough to sustain anything better than a subsistence nomadic existence virtually impossible.

In many parts of the world the whole system was drastically

modified by the development of technology which made it possible to exploit resources hitherto unuseable. Perhaps the most significant were the new sources of energy which at last gave independence from wood as the major structural and energy resource.

Technology, therefore, opened a completely new storehouse of resources and of course, the inevitable happened. Populations exploded in one country after another as they became industrialised. Medical science helped populations to grow even faster than they would have done anyway. As if that were not enough, the economists added their little bit by suggesting that labour meant wealth and with that characteristic leap of the imagination, for which economic theorists should be famous, they propounded that more people also equalled more consumption and, therefore, even more industry and wealth.

In this country we have been riding the crest of this wave for about 150 years. The population has been growing steadily to consume the resources of coal and iron ore which we were fortunate to find in the ground. We made a fortune from these resources in the nineteenth century, just as the oil producing areas of the Middle East are growing rich on their resources now. The exploitation of our resources gave us a lead in technical know-how which has made it possible for us to sustain the growth in population and standards of living long after the most easily available resources were used up.

But as far as the environment is concerned it has taken a very severe hammering, first from the development of technology and the production of energy in all its forms and, secondly, from a growing population with ever-increasing standards of consumption. Forty million more people have been accommodated in this small island during the last 150 years. The census taken in 1821 gives a figure of 15.5 million for the United Kingdom. In 1973 the figure is 55.5 million, and all enjoying a much higher standard of life. This may well represent a tremendous success in terms of human and material growth, but it has been achieved at considerable cost. I do not think we need slavishly accept that bigger is inevitably better.

This vast increase in the population alone has made a considerable impact on the environment, and if in addition, the average rate of consumption of resources and water and the production of waste per person has increased by something like 100 per cent in the same period, the impact is even more noticeable.

The first signs of anxiety appeared many years ago, but it is really in the last decade that a great many people began to notice what was happening. Ironically, they identified pollution and the exploitation of resources as the major causes of the degradation of the environment, and that just at the moment when resources were beginning to get a bit thin anyway, when the demand for energy was growing faster than ever, and worst of all, when the less developed countries are just beginning to enjoy the fruits of technology. Furthermore, as the populations of these less developed countries increase, so the exportable surplus of their agricultural products and eventually, of course, of their other resources is decreased.

It does not need a great stretch of the imagination to realise that if resources become scarce and demand continues to rise, prices are liable to go up. At this precise moment people concerned with the environment are very reasonably demanding that levels of pollution should be reduced and the exploitation of resources should be more carefully controlled. Desirable as they are, it is no good pretending that these demands will not increase costs to the consumer still further. We are indeed facing a classic situation from which only a co-operative effort can hope to extricate us.

I think the conservationists need to know more about the practical problems and alternatives of meeting the forecast energy requirements in these islands, while the energy industries need to know more about the actual and the threatened impact of their industries on the environment. It is worth remembering that the energy sector comprises the country's largest capital investment in industrial processes, with an annual turnover of £1,000 million and 700,000 people employed. Every household in the land is a customer for at least one of its products. Furthermore we cannot contemplate a halt to the improvement in the standards of living of the people of this country who are less well off.

This is going to require more horsepower available for people at work, and more therms for household use of all kinds. This will have to come from more power stations and more fuel to feed them, whether it be coal, oil, gas, nuclear or any other source which may be developed meanwhile. These stations will have to be sited somewhere, and faced with the inevitable we must use everything science and technology has to offer to reduce their impact on the environment.

It is, therefore, rather more important than usual to ensure that expenditure for environmental or amenity reasons is justified by a measurable or significant improvement or by the necessary protection of the health, home, factory, crops or amenity of the consumer or of what remains of our wildlife on land or in the waters.

Any discussion of the impact of the energy industries on the environment should take place against a background of exact facts and figures. But facts and figures are not the whole story. We face the far more difficult task of trying to define the sort of environment in which we want to live. It is bound to be a compromise because there is a limit to the material sacrifices which people are prepared to make simply for some abstract concept of conservation. It is a bit easier to define the amenities which people can appreciate for their own enjoyment. It is much less easy to define conditions under which the rest of the living world should be allowed to exist. These things are extremely difficult to quantify so that conservation is almost always on the defensive.

The ideal would be to say in advance exactly what needs to be preserved or protected, and this can be done in some cases, but more frequently the need to protect only arises in response to a specific threat. But either way we need the most exact estimates of the costs of protecting these amenities and of creating or preserving these conditions. Unless all these cards are put on the table it will be quite impossible to try to make any sensible assessment of the real problems which face us or to estimate some sort of priority in seeking their solution.

Conference on 'Fuel and the Environment'
EASTBOURNE, 27 NOVEMBER 1973

PART TWO
The Human Environment

The Countryside in 1970

1963

The word 'conservation' will probably be used fairly frequently during this conference and I think it is important that we should all use it in the same sense. I would like to suggest that we use it in its broadest sense, to mean the total management of the rural areas of this country for the fair and equal benefit of all groups which have a direct interest in their use.

This definition makes it quite clear, I hope, that conservation is not a polite way of attempting to put the clock back, nor is it an attempt to turn the countryside into an open-air natural history museum. This is not a campaign to fossilise the landscape. Any such attempt would be quite ridiculous considering that almost three-quarters of the land area of this country is under intensive cultivation.

Conservation means removing blemishes and creating new beauties and delights for the hard-pressed urban population. Economic and technical progress can still march on but turn aside from the most beautiful places and leave them undisturbed. It means that the machinery and structures of progress are harmonised in scale and outline and designed to cause less fuss, noise and disturbance. It means encouraging people to use the countryside intelligently and with understanding and loving care, leaving it as they find it. Which is far from being the case at the moment – I know from personal experience.

This Conference is really the culmination of a process which has been going on for a number of years. Certain groups of people have had an interest in nature and wildlife for generations but it is only recent years that have seen a really dramatic growth of interest in the countryside and wildlife.

Many conservation organisations have been established with one aim in view, frequently and quite naturally unaware that their policies and plans might cause difficulties for other equally worthy organisations. It is inevitable because there was bound to be a head-on collision between those with an interest in conservation, be it landscape, wild places, birds, animals, insects or plants; and those whose activities have a direct impact on nature, particularly modern agriculture, urban and industrial development. The most heartening aspect of this whole subject is the genuine and growing concern felt by those responsible for agriculture, urban and industrial development for the whole problem of the conservation of nature.

However it is obvious that this general concern can only be turned to good account if the conservation movement can speak with one voice and if it can make it clear what it wishes to conserve and why it wants to conserve it. There must be an overall concept of conservation to which all interested parties can subscribe. We must have a clear idea of the sort of countryside we want to see and experience in the '70s and, just as important, how this countryside is going to be used. This, as I see it, is the main theme of the Conference.

Opening Address, Study Conference 'The Countryside in 1970'
LONDON, 4 NOVEMBER 1963

1965

The first 'Countryside in 1970' Conference, in 1963, showed conclusively that there was a great deal of common ground between all the interests represented, and provided we could find a means of exploiting this willingness to co-operate there was a real hope that something valuable might be achieved.

This coming together of all the interests concerned with land use has happened at the last possible moment. The rate of change and development is so rapid that another few years without a meeting such as this would have seen widespread and irretrievable damage.

Conservation is not a matter of putting the clock back or of preserving things just because they exist. Conservation is much more a matter of intelligent planning so that we can bring about the sort of countryside and land use which we want to have. The pressure is so great and the variety of uses for which land is needed is so wide that restraint and compromise is inevitable.

There is sometimes a tendency to say that if only there was more money many problems could be solved. Money can certainly do a lot but it is no substitute for clear thinking and it is no alternative to sensible organisation.

The first need is to get the organisation right, responsibilities properly allocated, a framework for co-operation constructed, the proper legislation introduced and a sensible relationship between Government departments and between central and local government established. Then, and only then, need we discuss the spending of money.

Finally, I think we must be realistic about this whole subject. Whatever we do here and whatever is done as a result of these meetings, friction, disagreement and conflict in the use of land are inevitable.

Our main objective must be to create a structure and an atmosphere in which these problems can be sorted out or at least discussed without anger or abuse. Enthusiasts for any one point of view or activity cannot be expected to know by some sort of divine inspiration why their particular claims are not accepted immediately by everyone else. As most of them are fortunately intelligent people they are quite capable of seeing the other side of the argument when it is reasonably presented, and of reaching a sensible compromise if they have confidence in each other.

Second 'Countryside in 1970' Conference
LONDON, 10 NOVEMBER 1965

1970

The title 'The Countryside in 1970' was chosen in 1963 in an attempt to concentrate our thinking and planning on a fixed point in the future. Those seven years seem to have gone by very quickly, much too quickly in fact to allow us to achieve all our ambitions.

Seven years ago, information and facts about conservation were not easily come by and frequently none were available. To-day, people who want to know about these things can find out without difficulty. Even people who do not want to know about these problems can hardly avoid sensing the anxiety and concern all around them; they are at least conscious that something is wrong. There is a new awareness.

This new awareness has already had some important consequences. A much more critical attitude towards all types of land use has developed. Industrial and urban development, waste disposal, recreation, wildlife, agriculture and the use of agricultural chemicals have all come in for a much closer and better informed scrutiny.

In many cases, the industries concerned are taking a more active interest and, together with legislation, voluntary controls and statutory bodies, the most pressing problems are being tackled. Even the unconvinced have learnt to take conservation seriously.

The land of these islands has come to be recognised as our most valuable resource. It has now suddenly become apparent that water – clean, fresh water – is no longer in unlimited supply and that it too needs to be treated as a valuable resource and not squandered or wasted. The whole complicated cycle of collection, storage, distribution, drainage, sewage and the use of water for recreation and to sustain aquatic wildlife is at last under some sort of control, but further co-ordination will certainly be necessary.

The air we breathe has long been a source of trouble and, in recent years, complaints about its condition have resulted in serious and, in many cases, successful attempts to control smoke, smell and noise.

Behind all this, a discussion has been going on about pressures exerted by a steadily increasing population. There has been a questioning of the standard theory that a larger population means more consumption and more workers and therefore greater prosperity. It is now suggested that the best hope of providing adequate social services, employment opportunities, recreational facilities and a tolerable environment lies in maintaining a stable population.

In the years after the war, it was widely believed that science, technology and economic measures were the hope of the future; they were to be the great deliverers from drudgery and the promise of a Golden Age. Perhaps we put too much faith in them, perhaps we expected too much from this form of materialism.

Today, we recognise that they must be wisely controlled. At any rate, they too are now under scrutiny and people are beginning to count the cost of the massive technological developments which have taken place in the last fifty years in terms of the damage to human existence. No one denies the convenience of the gadgets and equipment which have been produced, but the side-effects are beginning to look extremely worrying.

The search for and exploitation of resources to feed this insatiable technological monster, the exploitation of human resources to manage it and the mountains of waste it produces all result in the gradual erosion of our whole living environment.

The situation in Britain, which prompted the first Countryside Conference in 1963, has turned out to be a part of an immense world-wide problem. What started as an exercise in co-operation to control abuses and plan development in our own countryside is now seen to be part of a much more extensive campaign to save the world from human exploitation.

The problem in 1963 was to discover what was wrong; the problem facing us today is how to put it right. There are two problems: first, we need to put our own house in order, and secondly, there is a desperate need for more effective international co-operation and action. There is still a long way to go, but it is surely encouraging that the members of the Council for Europe have found it possible in 1970 to sponsor European Conservation Year.

It is at least a start, but the solution of international problems is the same as the solution of national problems. It requires effective administrative organisation, capable of putting agreed policies into effect. Without an administrative structure able to take decisions and without an organisation designed to put those decisions into practice, there is no possibility of progress.

It is too easy to make estimates and to argue about the costs of protecting the environment. It is nothing like so easy to demonstrate the cost of a deterioration in the environment if we fail to take sensible conservation measures.

It is really quite unreasonable to put the cost of curing pollution against conservation. Pollution, in the first place, is the culprit and the losses it causes are even greater than the cost of cure.

The trouble is that conservation of the environment cannot be measured directly in economic terms. Indeed, whenever conservation gets into an economic argument, it is inevitably made to look as if it were opposed to all forms of economic development.

When a national park stands in the way of the exploitation of a natural resource, such as potash, for example, or a reservoir, the national interest measured in the economic terms of exports and balance of payments wins every time.

Economic advantage is easily measured in cash terms; social cost is just a figure of speech. The Gross National Product, which is rapidly assuming the religious significance of a graven image, can be worked out by any competent accountant, but exactly how do you arrive at a comparable figure for the quality of life?

The trouble is that conservation is a cultural, moral, ethical or even a religious issue. It is to do with belief and conscience, it is to do with future generations and the fate of the world as the habitat for all forms of life as we know it. It is not a matter of immediate profit and convenience.

The fact is that the subject of conservation has become a large and extremely awkward spanner in our well-oiled, materialist economic system. We have got to the point where we believe that every problem is an economic problem and if something can't be measured directly in terms of money, it just doesn't exist. Because conservation is a new and awkward problem, I suspect many people fondly hope that by ignoring it, the problem will quietly go away.

Unfortunately, the deterioration of the environment does exist for every observant individual to notice. It is not a figment of a crank's imagination or a communist plot or another phase in the class struggle or even a gimmick by the industrially advanced countries to stop the developing countries enjoying a higher standard of living.

The attempt to argue away unpleasant situations is a classic human characteristic and if that doesn't work, the next trick is to suggest that the problem is nothing like as serious as the alarmists would have us believe. Exaggeration is, of course, possible in both directions, but just because you would prefer an accidentally encountered elephant to be the size of a mouse doesn't actually make it so.

If argument and minimising fail, the next fall-back position is ridicule. If you can make enough fun of it, perhaps it will get embarrassed and look less menacing. Finally, if all else fails, the usual behaviour is to get into a panic and run away.

I believe we can do better than that. I believe that if we are sensible and rational about this, we can work out an arrangement which will allow us to keep the situation under control; we can establish an organisation with the necessary responsibility and executive powers and we can devise priorities and programmes of public information and research.

If the period of the last seven years has been one of discovery of the facts, I believe the time has come to think about the problems of conservation in a wider context. I believe we should attempt to form a comprehensive view of conservation, which sees each of the subjects to be discussed at this Conference as part of a greater whole. Each is a subject in itself, but each must be related to the other to form a coherent picture of the situation facing us in this country at present and to gain an idea of what may happen in the future.

Conservation problems are no more static than economic

problems. We know about the backlog of abuses which need to be corrected but, while we make the necessary corrections, new and unexpected problems will certainly appear. We will only be able to deal with past mistakes and future hazards if we can rely upon an effective system of warning, research and executive action.

Third 'Countryside in 1970' Conference
LONDON, 26 OCTOBER 1970

Enterprise Neptune

From the very earliest times the British have shown a particular concern for the beauty of their countryside. The rich laid out great parks and gardens, and the not so rich cultivated gardens on a smaller scale but no less brilliant in their colours. In few other countries are municipal parks and gardens so well cared for. Artists and poets have been more deeply stirred by the pure country of these islands than almost anywhere else in the world. It is this background of love and understanding which explains, I think, why the colonial territories were so well served by their British foresters, why their game parks have been handed on in such a flourishing condition, why their birds and plants have been catalogued and named as British, and why it was mostly amateur ornithologists, botanists and all the other collectors and watchers of nature who laid the foundations of the science of natural history in almost every country outside Europe. I may say that this picture of the slightly mad, but otherwise quite nice and harmless Englishman collecting beetles or bandying Latin plant names or watching perfectly familiar birds in most uncomfortable conditions is still very strong in a great many parts of the world. But the people of these islands were not just passive onlookers and appreciators of a country. They also used it actively for their pleasure and enjoyment. Almost every country sport and outside game had its origins in this country. And their English names have entered every language in the world. Others may beat us at these games or do better as professionals in natural history, but at least we can console ourselves that we invented them and anyway the main thing is to take part for the fun of it, rather than to win or to do anything so unpleasant as to make a living from them.

Now if you're feeling a bit like grinning with satisfaction all I can say is be prepared to wipe the grin off. Things are nothing like as rosy as they seem. Our beaches are getting crowded. Twenty million people use them annually. And in spite of the fact that the sands every year are getting more and more covered with oil. Our sailing areas are being invaded by industry and commercial shipping. The schoolchildren of London are lucky if they get one organised games period once a fortnight. Clubs have to queue up for their grounds. And there is a growing conflict between users for what is left of the water for fishing, for speed-boats, for cruising, for water skiing, for sailing, for underwater swimming, and for bird-watching. The national parks are being eroded by industry, and there is a mounting friction between those who wish to use the parks for different and clashing purposes. There is increasing exploitation as opposed to farming of agricultural and potential agricultural land. Marshes are being drained, mud-banks reclaimed, with the consequent loss to wild-bird and animal life. And if that isn't enough we've polluted the rivers to the extent that any form of life is inhibited. And we're also slowly becoming aware of the danger of polluting the country with partially understood chemicals.

Well that's what it's like today. Let's try and imagine what these things are going to be like by the end of the century, only thirty-five years from now. Our population is expected to increase by 37 per cent to some seventy million people. Private cars will increase four-fold to thirty-two million. The working week may be reduced to thirty hours. There is a good chance that real earnings for a major section of the population will also go up. The pressure on the land for the first priority, housing, and at a higher standard is going to become more severe. The second priority, somewhere to work, is also going to demand its share of the land area. Agriculture will inevitably become more industria-lised and less a compromise with nature. And new roads must also be squeezed in somehow. And into this pattern we must attempt to fit the facilities for recreation which a great proportion of a greater total population will expect. In fact, everything is growing and expanding except – most unfortunately – the physical dimensions of the British Isles.

This is very like the moment when a swimmer in difficulties begins to realise that there is a very good chance that he may drown. And again, like a swimmer in difficulties, any kind of support – anything which might help to gain even a temporary reprieve – is accepted with renewed hope and relief. And it is into this rather dismal situation that the National Trust has launched Enterprise Neptune. It is not a lifeboat, it is not the certainty of final rescue, but it is a burst of renewed hope, it is the lifebelt within reach, just that flash of inspiration and encouragement when the tired swimmer needs to keep afloat just a little bit longer. The essentials of the scheme are to acquire and preserve roughly one thousand miles of our coastline, about one-third of the coasts of England, Wales and Northern Ireland. Scotland has its own scheme.

The scheme is simple and given the necessary support there is no doubt that it could be immensely effective. It is not, and is not intended to be, comprehensive and all-embracing. It is specific to the coast. But the most important aspect is that it is thoroughly practical and businesslike.

The countryside and our coastline are the very fabric of our national existence, not just for today but for every succeeding generation. If we abandon that we might just as well abandon all the plans and expenses for a better standard of living. Because without some remnants of the countryside, which has inspired and warmed the hearts of generations of British people, life in these islands is going to be reduced to the level of animals on a factory farm. It may well be that this operation will be seen as a turning point in our whole approach to the problems of land use. And if this turns out to be the case, and this scheme is as successful as it deserves to be, countless millions of people and many future generations of our countrymen will have cause to be thankful to the National Trust, to Enterprise Neptune, and to all those who were sensible enough to support it.

'Enterprise Neptune' (*National Trust's Coastal Appeal*) *Luncheon*
MANSION HOUSE, LONDON, 11 MAY 1965

European Architectural
Heritage Year, 1975

1972

During roughly three thousand years the people of Europe have surrounded themselves with a quite remarkable range of buildings and structures and works of art and engineering. Until relatively recently none of this construction did more than make a modest impression on the natural environment, while the rate at which old and either beautiful or fascinating structures were knocked down for re-development was fairly leisurely, and quite a reasonable proportion escaped the process altogether.

Since the beginning of this century the growth in human population and the rate of new development in industry, housing and transport has been accelerating to a dramatic extent. The situation has been further aggravated by the appalling destruction caused by two World Wars.

It is now plain for the more observant people to see that the situation has reached a point where we have got to decide whether we are prepared to allow the process to continue unchecked and uncontrolled, or whether we want to retain some of the great works of previous generations against all the rules of economic viability or any of the other arguments which may be used to justify knocking down, breaking up and rebuilding.

I think we know what uncontrolled development means. We know about overpopulation, we know about pollution, we know about the dissipation of natural resources and we know how easy it is to knock down and rebuild. The prophets of doom may be exaggerating the dangers of following that alternative but I think it must be apparent that total collapse lies at the end of it sooner or later.

The other alternative is to grip the problem firmly now and to decide that we want to maintain the standards of all aspects of human existence to the best of our knowledge and experience and even if we are not quite able or quite ready with a complete plan for the future which we want to see, we can at least decide that there are a number of old, familiar or beautiful, or simply interesting things which we enjoy and which we believe future generations will enjoy as well. Planning for the future, of course, on a great scale is obviously a very complicated business involving a great many factors.

The campaign for the European Architectural Heritage Year in 1975 is concerned with one of the most important of those factors; the conservation of the best of our man-made environment, which means, amongst other things, the preservation of Europe's architectural heritage. It means the restoration and preservation of the great works of architectural engineering which bear witness to the genius of our predecessors, and I include engineering in this because I believe that what has come to be known as industrial archaeology fits into this campaign, particularly in this country as the home of the industrial revolution. And for reasons which should not be too obscure, I should also include historic ships which are after all the products of marine architects and just as much a part of our cultural heritage as many buildings ashore.

First meeting of the U.K. Council for the European Architectural Heritage Year, 1975
ST JAMES'S PALACE, LONDON, 21 DECEMBER 1972

1974

I think we are beginning to realise exactly how significant the whole concept of this campaign has been. We all accepted that it was a good idea, but I doubt whether anyone foresaw exactly how much could be achieved, how much interest could be created, how much satisfaction it could bring or what an important contribution it could make to our human environment.

For the first time since the beginning of the industrial revolution, the nation is being reminded of the long and gradual evolution of our civilisation. In preserving our heritage we cannot help but admire the people who created the things which give us so much pleasure today. If buildings reflect the spirit of their creators we should all feel a tingle of pride that we are descended from the people who were responsible for the towering cathedrals and the quiet village churches, for the great houses and the little cottages, for the grand architecture of the cities and for the comfortable market towns.

We are entitled to that pride, but we should also be feeling a chilling apprehension lest we do not do as well for those who will come after us. What we are doing now is only a beginning. Having had our conscience stirred we cannot let this new awareness simply die away and return to a grubbing expediency. It is no use simply trying to put our history into a museum, everything we preserve must remain part of our living existence and everything we build must fit into the continuity of our heritage. Just as the spirit of an age is reflected in its buildings so the spirit of our buildings is reflected in the people who live in them. The business of preservation, planning and building is much too important to be left to the experts and the professionals, we have all got to be involved in the creation of our environment. This campaign has demonstrated what public and community concern can achieve; this concern simply must continue.

Third meeting of the U.K. Council for the European Architectural Heritage Year, 1975
BANQUETING HALL, LONDON, 12 JULY 1974

1975

Not since the Renaissance or the early eighteenth century has there been such an interest in and such a concern for the architecture of previous generations, but even in those days there was nothing quite like the present campaign. I don't think there has been such an obsession with the natural and the built environment ever before and I believe it needs an explanation.

To begin with it is necessary to get our present situation into the right perspective. One hundred and thirty years ago the total population of England, Scotland and Wales was 18½ million. Of a total working population of 7 million, some 22.2 per cent were engaged in agriculture, 41 per cent in production industries and 18 per cent were in domestic employment. Transport was still virtually limited by the speed and endurance of horses and communications beyond the range of a good pair of lungs were no better.

Compare that with the present day. The population is 57 million. Of a total working population of 24½ million, 1.7 per cent are engaged in agriculture, 39 per cent in production industries and 0.4 per cent in domestic employment. Transport is entirely mechanised, except for a lunatic fringe which has translated horse-drawn transport into a sport. Towns and villages have had to accommodate a weight, volume and speed of traffic for which they were never intended while communications have been totally transformed by the electronic revolution which has produced telephones, radio and television.

All this represents the most radical technical, social, economic and environmental change ever experienced in the history of this or any other European country. It is not altogether surprising that there have been some quite dramatic consequences to the architectural heritage. Apart from anything else the biggest houses are uninhabitable because they are both too expensive and because they were designed for a completely different way of life. At the other end of the scale the houses which were built in a great rush to accommodate the rapidly expanding population of the last century do not meet the higher standards which modern technology has made possible.

Some 270 country houses have been demolished in England and Wales in the last thirty years and seventy in Scotland, and at the same time untold acres of what had become slum housing have been redeveloped. The better type of urban property may look the same from outside but there has been a complete change in the way it is occupied. Offices, hotels and flats have replaced family homes, while in the country, schools, golf and country clubs, safari parks, hospitals, museums, conference centres and old people's homes occupy the majority of the remaining country houses.

That has been the change in the physical, economic and social environment, but there has been an equally dramatic change in the intellectual environment. More has been discovered about the facts of life in the last fifty years than in the previous five thousand. Children at school are given the answers to questions and problems which previous generations could only guess at. They may be intrigued by other imponderables but things which were totally mysterious to their grandparents and even to their parents have been given quite commonplace explanations. Institutions which developed gradually over many centuries have been trying to adapt more or less willingly to a completely new set of circumstances.

All this has taken place in the life-span of three generations and I think it is amazing that it has not caused even more tensions and upheavals than we have witnessed in recent years. As far as the built environment is concerned it has produced some particularly difficult dilemmas. It is only natural to want to cling to the old and familiar, the graceful and the elegant, yet at the same time we want all the advantages of new technology. We want both the cultural and the convenient. Architects in particular have responded to the opportunities offered by new materials and new techniques. Consequently they have naturally come to see originality as more meritorious than quality, while costs and social demands have encouraged the functional rather than the aesthetic.

Perhaps the most important factor has been the ease and speed with which whole areas can be cleared and redeveloped. The projects can be designed on such a vast scale that the smallest mistakes become magnified into major social problems.

This country had nearly two thousand years to develop the material, social, economic and philosophical structure which managed to survive the buffeting of the late eighteenth and early nineteenth centuries. We are probably just coming to the end of two hundred years of industrial and scientific revolution and the world as we know it today, with its jets and television, computers and motorways, mass production and mass mobility has really only been with us for less than twenty years.

This means that everyone with a responsibility for the future – politicians in central and local government, planners and administrators, architects and educators, conservationists and developers, naturalists and industrialists – all have got to work within a completely new and strange set of constraints and pressures. This poses problems which glib theories, abstract doctrines or narrow sectional self-interests will do nothing to help to solve.

Our only chance is to remember some of the lessons which our predecessors learned with so much pain and bitterness. We must remember that no society can call itself civilised unless its individual members have a very large measure of freedom both to say and to do what they like within a liberal law. We must remember always to keep an objective view of human nature. We must create a living environment which suits people as they are at their best and not something based on an idealised view of what people ought to be. Above all we must remember that every society needs to be united by a sense of purpose and motivated by an ideal.

Nothing exerts such a powerful influence on the minds and behaviour of people as the built and natural environment in which they have their being. It is therefore vitally necessary to maintain the best of what we have inherited and to plan and build the best for the generations which will come after us.

Royal Institute of British Architects/Civic Trust Conference
'The Continuing Heritage'
QUEEN ELIZABETH HALL, LONDON, 28 JULY 1975

Three years ago we all set out to launch this great campaign to explain the need to protect and conserve Europe's architectural treasures. The campaign has given much-appreciated recognition to a very large number of conservation schemes undertaken by governments and other organisations. It has also given a very strong stimulus to the development of new plans and projects, many of which have been successfully completed during the course of the last three years.

The last thirty years have seen a considerable growth in radical political ideas in Europe and at the same time there have been tremendous technological developments. I believe this campaign has made it clear that the major threats to Europe's more recent architectural heritage have their origins in these two developments. Individuals have less wealth to spare for patronage of the arts while governments and industrial organisations can make use of the immense powers of modern technology to change the shapes of town and countryside virtually overnight.

I believe it is important to keep this in mind because the conservation and construction of towns and buildings are as much social and political as they are architectural and aesthetic problems. The buildings and structures which we want to conserve were the products of a living, creative, aspiring civilisation, but the conservation of these shells, to whatever new purpose they are put, is nothing more than the establishment of a museum culture. We talk about integrated conservation, which means preserving the past as well as providing a reasonable environment for contemporary life, but I am afraid this will turn out to be an illusion unless individuals feel that in addition to the importance of conservation there is also a positive encouragement to play their part in the improvement and development of a free and civilised society. The opportunities may be different but the motives must remain the same.

The whole purpose of the campaign has been to show the need to conserve and protect the architectural heritage, yet I believe we must be very careful to see that the preservation of historic towns and buildings does not come to be regarded as a creative activity in itself. Inevitably the legislation, finance and control of conservation will be in the hands of governments or their agents and the danger is that these great powers may well develop a bureaucratic paternalism over all the expressions of the human creative genius and skill.

While it is only natural to admire and to take pleasure in restored historic towns and buildings they will always remain the products of their creators and of their time. They are the response of identifiable people to the classic urge for perfection inspired by the freedom which European civilisation has always given to men of intelligence, originality and vision.

We must certainly preserve their creations but if we want new creations of the same standard we must also stimulate ambition and provide new opportunities for creative genius.

If we, in our generation, just sit and stare at these works or walk round them in a daze as if they were as inevitable as the mountains, without understanding that we are a part of the same stream of history, or without feeling inspired to make our own contribution in the same tradition, the whole purpose of conservation will be lost and our campaign will have been a waste of time.

It may not be possible for every individual to participate in all the complicated decisions which this modern age demands, but it is possible for everyone of us to participate in the continuing development of our European heritage and civilisation.

Congress on European Architectural Heritage
AMSTERDAM, 24 OCTOBER 1975

Restructuring Our Cities

It seems to be symptomatic of this aptly named industrial age that far more time and argument is devoted to industrial relations and the problems of people at work than to local government and to the problems of people at home. I am sure there are many others but there would appear to be three major factors responsible for the difficulties which are facing all big cities. The first was the general migration from country to town. The relative advantages and the greater opportunities of industrial, as opposed to rural, employment seem to be the main attraction, but there are obviously others such as the better social and cultural services usually available in cities and the inevitable concentration of commercial and administrative functions and the opportunities they provide.

When makes it all so perverse is that no sooner have people rushed in to enjoy the glamour of a city and made a success than they promptly rush out again to settle in the suburbs, where they long for the peaceful and uncomplicated life of the country. This suggests that in order to get the best of both worlds, more medium-sized cities would be preferable to just a few vast and slowly strangling conurbations.

The second factor would seem to be modern methods of transport. No sooner had the migration of workers and administrators swollen the cities to an intolerable extent, than the road system was struck by a transport explosion brought on principally by the personal motor car. To be more exact it is an explosion every evening and an implosion every morning as the suburban dwellers commute to and from their homes and places of work.

I suspect the third factor has been the tendency of so many of a city's traditional occupations to become industrialised. Small businesses of all kinds, shops, workshops, butchers, bakers and candlestick makers have all been displaced by factories, supermarkets, and department stores. The self-employed citizens, who used to be the backbone of the civic organism and the mainspring of the corporate civic pride and conscience, have become commuting employees and their homes are frequently outside the city limits. I hasten to add that their successors are just as worthy and probably more able, but attitudes are bound to be different.

All this has produced some fearful dilemmas. For a start, we all know what sort of standards of living we would like to see established in cities but the trouble is that ambition has simply overtaken our capacity to pay the cost. It really is no good turning to central government as if it were some sort of magic money fountain. Difficult as it may be to achieve, ambitions have got to be realistically related to the ability and willingness of citizens and their businesses to pay the price. And in the modern city structure, it is of course a double price because the convenience and comfort of living in the suburbs and working elsewhere doubles the infrastructure of municipal services which need to be supplied. With the traditional perversity of the individual citizen throughout the ages, he wants to have his private cake and enjoy eating it at the public expense.

Then what about the need for improved transport facilities and roads? It should be apparent that the better these are the worse the problems for the inner cities. The further people separate their houses from their industrial, commercial or administrative places of work the worse the traffic problems become. Furthermore, expenditure on transport is inclined to favour the better off at the expense of much needed urban renewal of poorer districts and the improvement of their municipal services.

The trouble seems to be that we have inherited city structures which were developed for entirely different patterns of life and work; and the problem facing all civic authorities is how to restructure the cities so as to accommodate modern patterns of living, travelling and working. I realise that any idea of deliberately changing the shape and structure of cities raises mind-boggling problems, but the fact is that, with or without thirty years of planning, their structure has been changed without any deliberate intent and we have fetched up with a thoroughly unsatisfactory compromise between the traditional concept of a city and the reality of modern living techniques.

Perhaps we should make city centres much smaller and restrict them to purely cultural and perhaps administrative functions. We could then accept that the suburbs are the real inhabited areas and, in order to prevent them sprawling all over the place, they might be ringed by employment facilities and all the components of the social infrastructure of schools, hospitals and shops. In other words, turn cities inside out and break them up into manageable component parts. It might then be possible for the parts to co-operate to manage the common centre rather than the other way round.

Perhaps we ought to question the need of quite so many people to have to do their work all together in huge factories concentrated in one part of the city and huge offices in another. With modern methods of transport and communications it should be much easier and cheaper to take work to and from people rather than taking people to and from work. Is some sort of a modern version of cottage industry including office work quite unthinkable? Of course this is not suitable for the final assembly phase of manufacture, but then is it really necessary to concentrate manufacture of components and assembly work under one roof? Smaller units need be neither noisy nor offensive in any other way and could therefore be more closely integrated into living areas.

I notice that size and rates of growth still seem to be matters of pride with civic authorities. Is bigger really always better? And growth produces hideous problems when it stops. I appreciate that the attraction of a larger income is very strong, but the costs are likely to increase in proportion, or why is it that so many of the biggest cities are facing the prospect of going bankrupt? And financial bankruptcy doesn't seem to be the only hazard of sheer size. Management problems, the involvement of individuals in decision-making, and human frustrations and tensions within a vast population are all aggravated by size.

The criterion of size should be what is humanly and practically manageable and not what is theoretically the most economical. The penalties of oversized cities are becoming increasingly obvious, but the cure is just as difficult as it is for those individuals who are overweight. The fact is that megalopolis is a disease.

Of one thing I am quite convinced. Drifting along in the hope of being bailed out by growth and at the mercy of an almost mindless migratory system and then complaining about the inevitable escalation in costs is unlikely to produce a satisfactory human cultural environment. No city of any size has achieved it yet and the chances of achieving it in the future are even slimmer.

Conference of Capital Cities' Lords Mayor
BRISBANE, 10 MARCH 1977

People and Their Environment

The word 'environment' isn't new. It has been in the dictionary for a very long time, but it is literally only in the past ten years that it has become more or less generally used. And the word has been associated more particularly with the natural environment, ever since people began to realise that there was a certain amount of difficulty about it. It started fifteen or twenty years ago when it became apparent that the use of only partly understood agricultural chemicals in pest control, and that sort of thing, was having rather undesirable side effects. Warning was given of this, but it took a little time to penetrate, because it is only people in the country and people directly to do with it who notice these effects.

The now famous book by Rachel Carson, *Silent Spring*, started people thinking about what they were doing to their environment and they started to look at other factors which were changing the face of the earth. It very soon became clear that so-called reclamation of wetlands, marshes, draining of lakes, cutting down of forests, development of agricultural areas and so on – together with the tremendous building programmes, the use of land for occupation and for development generally – reservoirs, storage dams and motorways – the whole physical development which has been taking place all over the country, and on top of that the commercial exploitation of wild populations, particularly in the sea – the feeling that the fish are there, and that all you've got to do is take them: that all of these things were beginning to encroach on areas which up until then were occupied by wild animals and wild plants. There was an anxiety about this particular aspect, in other words the disappearance of wild animals and places due to the encroachment of the human population.

Then people began to scratch their heads about not just the effects of noxious chemicals but about pollution, inadvertent pollution in the air, in the water and on the earth, in the soil. Probably the best example of the state of air pollution which this country reached were those pea-soup fogs we used to have. The Clean Air Act has virtually stopped those fogs in the centre of London, and has increased the sunshine which now penetrates into urban centres. But the effluent from industrial chimneys on the east coast – now measurable because techniques of measurement are so much better – gets carried across the North Sea and is deposited on Norway and Sweden.

You know as well as I do that we have been using our rivers as a combination of sewage disposers and rubbish tips, as industrial suppliers and effluent carriers. We want fish from them and we want to drink the water that goes through them. In fact our treatment of the whole of our natural supply of water has been quite appalling and we have killed a number of rivers stone dead and denied the use of this water to ourselves which we so desperately need.

On the soil we suspect that we have been putting a lot of things into it and are not altogether sure what effect they have. I think that we are now slowly beginning to realise that we have got to be a little more careful. We may be doing things which are not quite so reversible as merely converting the fog into clear weather.

It was becoming apparent that so much of this was due to technical developments which were taking place so fast that there was really no time to study the side effects before the damage occurred. It also became apparent, on top of the pollution problem, that the sheer size and the rate of growth of the human population throughout the world is creating an immense burden on this planet Earth. People started working out the statistics and it became clear that with a finite earth's surface, with finite resources of the most basic kind, that is air and water and food, the world could not sustain this rate of growth indefinitely. We cannot increase the land surface appreciably and we certainly cannot go on taking away every available acre for the occupation of people or taking it away from our fellow creatures, merely ending up with a kind of concrete jungle and a lot of domestic animals.

We have come to think that everything is solvable in economic and material ways, and suddenly we are pitchforked into this very unpleasant situation of having to make a moral judgement. We have got to decide from a purely moral or religious point of view what we are going to do about this situation, our situation, the human situation, in this country and in the world as a whole. From a practical and economic point of view we can say, 'Well, let's do away with all the wild animals, let's get rid of all the pests, let's cut down all the forests, let's develop every acre of land, let's occupy it for our benefit.' This is the material and economic answer. The problem that we are facing now is something rather more difficult. It is a moral and religious problem as to how we see our situation on this earth. We are now up against it, we have got to make a very important decision.

You see, one of the ironic things is that by assuming that everything is solvable by economic and material means, we have this weird situation that after twenty years' work by the World Health Organisation and the Food and Agricultural Organisation of the United Nations, there are more undernourished people and more people starving than there were before these programmes were started. This is no reflection on the work they have done. It is merely a reflection on their success, the success of keeping more people alive. If there is always 1 per cent who are going to be starving, 1 per cent of ten million is a great deal more than 1 per cent of two million. In total numbers you may not be solving as many problems as you think you are.

In this country alone a few simple calculations will show the sheer size of the social problem which we would have to be coping with if the estimate of twenty million increase in the population in the next thirty years was correct. If you come to think of it, twenty million people is two cities the size of London and we haven't got London right, let's face it, let alone anywhere else. To think that we can embark on this sort of programme with the limited resources that we have now, having used most of them up, is ridiculous. Let us also face another thing; we may have made ourselves reasonably prosperous by the brilliance of the population but an awful lot of prosperity came from digging things up out of the ground, like coal and iron ore and things like that which were needed. Anybody can be prosperous if they have a goldmine in their backyard. But what happens when you have run out of the gold?

So we would be confronted not only with a reduction of resources, which would make it possible to supply this enormous extra population, we would have to earn the resources, and we would have to earn the resources in order to buy food for the extra population from a world which, as we know, is under-nourished already. So we are taking away nourishment from people who need it more than we do. The sheer social problem of catching up – in housing, education and health – without this extra burden, is quite difficult enough. A very simple problem is supplying water to the existing population in a rational way without doing a lot of damage to our structure and lasting damage to the whole of our river system.

This brings me to the problem of the physical environment that people live in, their homes and schools and hospitals and playing fields and recreation centres and all the other species in the concrete jungle, this whole background to urban existence. This is after all what the majority of this country live in and appear to want to live in, judging from the rapidity with which they move out of the country into the towns. To most of them, and quite rightly, the most important and certainly the most immediate environment is this urban environment and not the world of nature. The first environment which anybody comes across in life is the environment of their home, and we all know only too well that everything isn't quite as it should be in housing in this country. There are many lovely churches and houses and gardens and much new and very effective development, and the best of these we ought to be concerned about conserving, but there are still too many homeless people. There are too many in substandard houses and there are also many too many places of work that are a disgrace. The environment that matters is not only the environment in the home. Of course you should have carpets and comfortable furniture and pictures and such things, but you don't switch off your aesthetic sense when you step out of the front door. After all, everybody has got to use the streets as much as they use their own homes and when you think that people probably spend more of their waking hours at their places of work than they do at home, this is an environment which is more obvious and more apparent and more permanent than anything at home. This we know is not as good as it ought to be.

There are too many crumbling schools, too many inadequate hospitals. There has been, and it is still going on, a tremendous redevelopment of the slums and city centres, but you have only got to travel around to see that there is really too much derelict land, there are too many acres suffering from blight. In fact, the immediate physical environment, for too many people in this country, is nothing like as good as it should be or as it could be, and if anything ever qualified for the term 'social service' then any attempt to improve, to clean up and to modernise our physical environment qualifies for that term.

The changes which the world – the more industrialised world – has had to face in the last hundred years are unique in human history. Nothing quite like this has happened before and nothing quite like this will happen again. For instance in transport, in one generation people have gone from horses to supersonics and in the same generation communications have gone from messengers with a cleft palate to radio and television. All these changes have taken place in the span of one or perhaps two generations, and these technical changes have put a tremendous strain on the people who have lived through them. With every new development you have to re-adjust. People who thought they were going to live out their lives in one set of conditions find that half-way through their lives they are confronted with a different set of conditions. They think that they are settled in one way and they are unsettled a moment later. In order to survive at all people have to adapt in a very remarkable way.

Changes may be better for some – and for many they are, of course, better, don't let's delude ourselves. I think the technical developments, the technological advances which have been made have generally been reflected in a very much better standard of living for a very large number of people. Don't let's mistake that for one moment, but don't also let us forget that all changes cause a good number of casualties. So that instead of screaming abuse at each other, let's at least recognise that we are all confused and that we are all looking for ways to come to terms with this new situation, with these new environments. It's not only the young who see anomalies and injustices in human nature and in the structure of human society. I think an awful lot of people see these difficulties and these contradictions. They are new problems or perhaps just old problems in a new form, and as a result of this the old solutions are no longer effective.

For that reason we need patience and co-operation and a combined effort to cope with this new situation. We've all got to help each other to get forward and to come to terms with these new environments. You may feel that we are living through the disappearance of what many held very dear, but you've got to look on the other side of it; there is also an opportunity to build for the future, just as so many of our most satisfactory towns and cities have developed over the ages, not by being destroyed, but by the contribution which each generation has made to their life and to their structure. I am sure that we can build on to the best of the existing features of those environments. I believe we can build new structures which are adapted, better adapted, to the present and future situation.

Annual General Meeting, National Council of Social Service
LONDON, 25 NOVEMBER 1970

Man at Work – the Next Fifty Years

When it comes to understanding human nature and getting the best out of people, there is really very little which has not already been discovered and tried. The problem here is to gather the evidence and experience of history and to arrange it in a comprehensive and useful form, so as to pass it on to the next generation. After all, one of the worst problems that we have to face is that every generation is born totally ignorant and its future depends entirely on what it learns and how quickly it learns it.

An analysis of the present is probably more difficult because every change in the human environment creates a new situation. The basic factors may remain the same, but they become re-arranged and acquire different values. The introduction of industrial manufacture, for instance, completely changed the whole situation of man at work and we are really still working out the consequences of that change. However fascinating and important the industrial system may be, it shouldn't blind us to the fact that industry and work as a whole are only means to an end, or means to ends, and not ends in themselves. It is worth remembering that industry itself is only one form of work and different in many important respects from, say, agriculture, catering or distribution, although people do tend to call them industries. Man is primarily a citizen and not a worker. Work, and the way it is organised, needs to be seen in relation to man in his community, at home and in his family. In the same way, industry must be seen as a part of and a service to the community, rather than the purpose of the community. And this applies even when a community is set up specifically to exploit a particular process or a natural resource. Now, if you carry this argument a stage further, you can begin to discuss all sorts of interesting problems, like the social merits of cottage industry, for instance, where you move the materials to and fro instead of the people. You leave them where they are.

The important point about any analysis is that it should be based on facts and not assumptions. The trouble is that when the facts themselves are based on human opinions, it is rather like trying to pin down a will-o'-the-wisp. I suppose this is why so much of our present management, whether industrial or economic, is plagued by theories which are based, very often, on false or wishfully thought-out assumptions. It seems to me that too many people feel that things ought to be like this or that, or that people ought to feel this way or that way. The difficulty is to be sure that exactly what they think and feel has been discovered. And even answers to questionnaires may not always give the true answer. If and when this has been achieved, the next problem is, of course, to act upon it – and to act upon it even if it contradicts the most strongly held beliefs and theories. I sometimes believe that this is an even more difficult hurdle.

When it comes to predicting the future, it is really a case of stating the options and offering the choices. In effect, any prediction can only say that the consequences of the present situation will be so and so, and the consequences of this action will be so and so, and the consequences of that action will be like that and hope that every factor has been taken into consideration and given its right value. The most obvious situations which are causing problems at the present time are population increase, pollution and industrial development. Each of these reacts on the other but, unless we do something fairly drastic and fairly soon, the consequences of the present situation do not appear likely to be in the best interests of human civilisation as a whole.

One of the consequences of scientific and technological development has been that, whether we like it or not, we are now fully in control of virtually every feature of our environment. We can actually choose whether to destroy it by default or incompetence or greed, or to save it by considered action. This means that any alternative courses of action are not sufficient if they are merely concerned to correct what appears to be dangerous in our present situation. They must also relate the consequences to some long-term ideal. In fact, they must have in mind the best interests of the human civilisation as a whole. I think it is at this point that the scientific method is no longer any real help. This is where value judgements come in and where morality begins to play a part. By that I don't mean the morality created by expediency, but the morality which is compounded of experience, of reason and of hope. A morality, in fact, which every philosophy and every religion has tried to create for mankind so that men can have some point of reference in their reaction both to their own nature and to the world they find around them.

Golden Jubilee Conference, National Institute of Industrial Psychology
CONGRESS HOUSE, LONDON, 16 NOVEMBER 1971

Health and the Environment

Having listened to what was said at this meeting* has raised a great many more questions in my mind than it has answered, so that my summing up – at least most of it – will really be telling you more or less the questions raised in my mind rather than what I think the solutions are.

We listed the environmental factors, the chemical agents in agriculture and industry and society and medicine, as the things most affecting the human environment, but I think that we've got to take the total human environment into account when we're talking about health. It includes the physical conditions of life, the physical conditions of community, housing, work and recreation, and human relationships and, of course, the total medical environment and the effect all this has on the mental state of individuals, of families and of the community. I think we all wholly agree that medical services have been more concerned with preserving life than with health and that they are orientated more towards cure than towards prevention. But don't forget that the need for cure was there very much earlier and was much more obvious than the need for prevention. I think a lot of the things we were talking about demonstrated that the concept of prevention is becoming much more important, particularly the control of the environment.

A very important point which was discussed in considerable detail was the increasing population. If you have an increasing population your social infrastructure in education, health services, housing and so on, will never catch up. We know, as it is, that in

* Of the Edinburgh Medical Group.

spite of an increasing education budget in, say, India, the increase in population is such that the rate of literacy is actually going down.

The population is both a cause itself of environmental deterioration and also, if you come to think of it, a result of scientific and medical activity. The results of an increasing population are not necessarily increased economic standards; in many cases it's the very reverse. But, of course, if you reduce the number of deaths and increase the population, in an area where the resources are still limited, all you have is an increased population to use up the same resources, which means that there is a general lowering of standards.

The other thing we ought to bear in mind is that the control of population has always been by two factors: one, the availability of food and two, the standard of health. If you remove both these restraints at once, you get all sorts of difficulties. For instance, Britain is the third most densely populated country in the world, with 606 people per square mile. And if you take England alone, it's the most highly populated area in the world, with 920 people per square mile. The net increase today of our population is something like 300,000 every year, or 600 people a day,* which means 600 new jobs a day – at a time when we've got a quite high unemployment rate and this is being added to it. On top of that, we need 400 new houses a day and a new school every day.

If this human population is not going to become a plague, it's got to be restricted in some way, and preferably voluntarily. Economists always like to point out that if you stop the growth in population, you increase the proportion of old people and, therefore, you decrease your ability to earn a living and everything goes to hell. I just wonder whether this is really much worse than the situation they have to face in Brazil, where 48 per cent of the population is under fourteen. I think that when it comes to deciding what the optimum population of a country is, it may be old-fashioned, but I suggest that it should be limited to what it can feed.

* The actual figure is about 730 for the decade 1961–71.

If you keep everything alive, everybody alive, are we in fact in danger of reversing the process of natural selection? It works extremely slowly in the beneficial sense: in the selection of what are good qualities or useful qualities or qualities which are, perhaps, helping people to survive in the environment. If you suddenly give everything that is born an equal chance of survival, are you not then reversing the process of natural selection?

A corollary to this is the extent to which the Government – our collective responsibility – should protect the human environment by the control of the pollution of air, land and water. But this time at the expense of industry and development. It is possible to be absolutely clean, but what happens to our ability to compete in world markets? How can we make a living if we've made it so expensive to manufacture that we won't then have anything to export? Amenity for all may mean unemployment for all, which is just as difficult. The problem of intervention in industry is very real and it applies both to existing industries, that is the extent to which we can clean up practices which are current at the moment, and even more important, the extent to which we intervene in the development of new industries. I think this is the most difficult dilemma of all and the essence of the problem is the argument between development and conservation: the argument between the ecol-nuts against the econ-nuts. Until we have the vision and the ambition for a future life, conservation will always lose by default because development is always expedient and is always in the national interest. It's much more difficult to reduce conservation to the sort of statistical proof which a lot of people seem to need.

Everybody seems to think this is a new problem. If you look back, you'll find that all the ancient civilisations came unstuck over exactly the problems we're discussing now. They didn't have the same resources, but when they used up the resources that they had, the civilisations came to an end. You've only got to look around at the big deserts of this world to see that they really did exhaust their resources. The situation is exactly the same, only the resources available to us are different. Don't forget that the controls on the population – the natural controls – are exactly the same today as they were then. If there's a limitation in food and a limitation in health, that limits the population. If you remove those, they go up. Unless we can jointly and deliberately decide that these natural controls are not going to operate because we don't want them to operate. We can only do this if we really become aware, both of the problems and of what they are likely to lead to. On top of that, I think, we must have a vision of the sort of place we would like to live in, or that we would like our children and our grandchildren to live in.

Edinburgh Medical Group meeting on 'Health and the Environment'
EDINBURGH, 17 DECEMBER 1971

The Earth is Our Home

The conditions under which people live and work have always attracted a lot of interest. There have been rules about making smoke, laws about light and controls on the use of river water since time immemorial.

The more recent excitement is largely due to the discovery that a number of the activities of modern scientific man are having a very marked effect on the world's wild populations of animals and plants. We discovered, for instance, that agricultural chemicals were making survival next to impossible for large numbers of birds and beasts. We found that certain compounds were making birds sterile; we found traces of these compounds in animals which lived remote from man.

We discovered that the cutting of forests, the draining of swamps and the exploitation of mineral resources were destroying wild habitats. We found that the water of rivers and estuaries was being polluted by effluents which poisoned fish and other aquatic creatures. Then, to everybody's general amazement, we discovered that the fogs of industrial centres like London were largely man-made and that they could also be lethal to man.

After that it was not very long before people began to realise that the increase in the demand for food and raw and urban effluents, and for the disposal of waste, are directly due to the human population explosion.

What started out as concern for wildlife has rapidly become a concern for human life. While it is not exactly easy to make the survival of wildlife much more than an abstract concept for most people, it is relatively simple to get people to be concerned about the quality of their own survival. The result is that the future of human life on the earth is seen to be threatened by three things; the human population explosion which, if continued unchecked, at the present rate will obviously grossly overpopulate the limited land area of this earth. Secondly, the present increasing rate of exploitation and consumption of non-renewable raw materials which must ultimately exhaust the world's reserves. Thirdly, pollution due to the increasing human population and the rapid development of industry.

So far so good. There may be disagreements about the time scale, but in principle there can be little doubt that the population cannot go on increasing indefinitely; resources presently being used will not last for ever and pollution in its broadest sense, unless severely checked, is bound to increase with population and industrial activity.

The reall discussion begins with the problem of how to react to this situation and what, if anything, can and should be done about it. The idea of population control, after thousands of years trying to survive, is a concept which many people find almost impossible to comprehend. Even if it is comprehended, the practical difficulties are daunting, so that it is not surprising that so many people shrug their shoulders and escape the issue by saying 'something will happen'. The trouble is that things 'have happened' before, which effectively limited or reduced populations, and they have always been extremely unpleasant for those who experienced them. I cannot really imagine anyone in this day and age advocating famine, pestilence or war as a satisfactory method of population control.

The exploitation of presently used non-renewable resources produces two reactions. There are the optimists who claim that recycling and resource substitution will put off the crisis indefinitely. However, it is difficult to see how even this solution can cope with the natural demand, particularly by those large numbers who are less well off, for standards of living more or less comparable with the best available. The other reaction is to suggest restriction of consumption which is equally difficult to visualise in practice. This doctrine of 'I'm all right Jack' is hardly likely to commend itself to those who are not all right.

Pollution also generates two completely opposed attitudes. The optimists say that it can be controlled by better technology, although they admit that it will be at a price. The opposite view is that as pollution is caused by technology and industry, the way to beat pollution is to restrict the activities of technologists and industrialists. It doesn't take a great leap of the imagination to see that this sort of cure might simply make the disease even worse.

The population problem is, of course, a personal and social issue, although obviously medical science can make a very important contribution. Pollution can certainly be controlled, but it will need a combined attack by legislation and better technology. However, the issue which science and technology can do most to resolve is the matter of resources. We desperately need other sources of energy; we know they exist in theory but it will need some exceptionally brilliant work to make them available in practice. That is probably the first priority, but the whole field of recovery and recycling of materials and resource substitution is wide open to scientists and technologists. Solutions cannot be found too soon. In my opinion this work must go ahead with the greatest possible urgency, while we still have time.

There are certain things in this life which are common to all occupations and professions and one of them is the natural environment. Some people, by their work and activities, have more effect on it than others, but the earth is our home, it is what we all have to live in, and the quality of the natural environment, which we bequeath to the next generation, depends upon the attitude of every single one of us, whatever we do for a living and whatever we do with our leisure.

University of Salford Degree Ceremony (2)
SALFORD, 16 JULY 1973

The Environment
and Human Satisfaction

Considering that from the very earliest of human civilisations, men have been attracted to live in what are now described as conurbations, it might well be asked what useful purpose this symposium can possibly serve. Is there anything about modern cities which is so radically different from Babylon, Rome or Constantinople? They must have been even more crowded and it is very unlikely that they were healthier or freer from crime. As far as their natural environment was concerned, their exploitation of the forests left the world with a legacy of huge deserts which are still with us today. Surely, it might be said, everything that needs to be known about the environment and human satisfaction is already known. All that needs to be done is to avoid making the same mistakes over and over again.

In fact, of course, there are many similarities between the past and the present, but there are also very great differences. In the first place, the sheer speed at which industrial technology has developed has meant constantly changing patterns of employment, personal mobility and social structures. Secondly, the wealth created by new resources and new methods of production resulted in the inevitable growth of population. Taking this country as an example, forty million people have been added to the population in the short space of 150 years. In that same period the whole new process of industrial mass production was devised and introduced, and has become the basis of our existence and the means of national subsistence. These alone would have put almost unbearable strains on any society – but that was not the end of it.

We have converted from an agricultural and craft society to an industrial urban society. We have gone from a non-mechanical to a mechanical way of doing things. We have converted from a very loosely organised system of government to a tightly controlled bureaucratic structure. All in all, the structures we have created have become too big, too complex and too violent. All these changes have created as many and more complex problems than they have solved, largely because they have all happened so quickly. With a rapidly growing population and an insatiable demand for manufactured goods, houses and factories were naturally more urgent than aesthetics or environmental considerations. It is only within recent times that the consequences of all these developments and the legacy of social and material changes have made themselves apparent, and it is even more recently that people have begun to realise that the disadvantages of dissatisfied communities outweigh the advantages of growth at any cost.

I believe we have a special brand of problem today, simply because it is possible to tear down and reconstruct so quickly and on such a vast scale. One team of local authority officials, planners, architects and constructors can design and build all the material requirements for a community of tens of thousands of total strangers within a few months. Things very often go right, but if there are any mistakes they are made on a grander scale than ever before, and the team responsible merely goes away to its own homes leaving the new community to get on with it as best they can. The plans are certainly made with the very best intentions but the construction of all the buildings necessary to create a satisfactory human community is by far the most difficult and complicated task that any group of people – no matter how well-intentioned – can ever undertake. The construction of new towns or new housing estates and all their infrastructure of employment, transport, recreation, health care, education, entertainment, and all the other vital factors, has seen the destruction of more shining theories and bright dreams than any other human activity. It should be apparent by now that this subject is too important to be left to the theories and experiments of philosophical speculators.

The truth is that it is almost impossible to create communities for other people. Building for people is not like building a zoo for animals. People must be able to create their own environment for themselves and the inhabitants must continue the unending process of adjusting and improving it. That is what participation really means. They may make more small mistakes than the bureaucratic Big Brother, but they will be responsible for what they do and they will have to live with their mistakes as well as enjoy their successes.

This symposium is inevitably an academic exercise, but that does not mean that it is only of academic interest. The academic contribution to the creation and maintenance of satisfactory human communities is absolutely vital, even though it may seem to have a slightly negative quality. The essential value of the academic element is the identification of mistakes through study and comparison. If communities are to have the power to create and manage their own environments they must have help in avoiding what are known to be mistakes. This may sound a bit limited, but if you come to think of it there can never be a perfect blueprint for success in the construction of human communities, for the simple reason that human satisfaction with the environment defies definition; whereas dissatisfaction, in the form of social diseases, such as crime, vandalism, drunkenness and violence, is immediately apparent. The essential need is to identify and prevent the causes of these diseases.

We have had doctors to treat individual cases since time immemorial, what we need now are doctors capable of diagnosing and prescribing for the social diseases from which so many urban industrial communities are obviously suffering. These doctors need the same scientific basis for their training as the general practitioner – a modern version of witch doctors would be worse than useless.

University of Salford, symposium on 'The Environment and Human Satisfaction'

SALFORD, 24 MAY 1974

PART THREE

Man in His Environment

The Evolution of Human Organisations

Within the last two hundred years a great shift in human thought has been taking place. Sometimes described as the scientific revolution, it is the sudden and rapid discovery of facts. Facts about the world and the universe, facts about growth and death, substances and processes, about the stars and about the weather. Suddenly we know about things which all previous generations could only guess at. Things which used to seem mysterious and frightening suddenly have very ordinary explanations.

This explosion of facts has only just started, there is much more to come, particularly facts about man himself. Already the workers in demography, sociology, anthropology, psychology and economics have uncovered great stores of facts, but man is a greater problem than the sum of these parts. Furthermore, it will need much more than these sciences working in isolation if we are to use this knowledge to improve human organisations. The population explosion is not just a demographic issue, it is probably the most important factor in the future of the world's economic structure as well.

The discovery of facts by the use of thought has made possible the new technological environment in which we now live, with all the material gadgets and comforts on which each generation becomes more dependent.

Whereas the power of thought had up till now only produced a new environment for man's intellect, the revolution in science and technology has created a totally new physical as well as intellectual environment. The newly discovered facts have in part upset some of the ideological concepts, but more important, they have changed, and are still changing, our whole pattern of existence. Modern transport is changing the structure of towns and cities and the way people live; modern industry is changing the pattern of employment and the social structure. Equally important, modern methods of communication have produced a revolution as profound as the development of the alphabet or the invention of printing.

This greatly increased factual knowledge is now a third layer in our human make-up. The first is the primitive behaviour patterns, the second is the reasoned thought which has produced such concepts as love, justice and liberty,★ and now the third layer, a vastly increased knowledge of facts and a new awareness of the human situation.

Unfortunately the layers are not of an equal thickness in each person or group. The less any individual exercises his ability to think, so much the less will he be influenced by the results of reasoned thought. If an individual does not bother to grasp the discovered facts about our existence, he cannot possibly become aware of his own or the human situation as a whole. So that if the second layer of human thought and the third layer of know-ledge are both rather thin, then quite obviously the first layer of primitive behaviour patterns is proportionately much thicker and has, therefore, a greater controlling influence. In which case reactions to particular situations should be more or less predict-able.

Up till now human organisation has depended upon one of two approaches. It has either been a purely empirical approach governed by only half-understood urges and emotions, or one of pure logic which is probably even further divorced from human needs. It is really a question of looking at our existence in the new light of ascertainable fact.

Perhaps I can make this more obvious by offering some examples. One of the most vital needs among men today is to make a living and to retain a job. It is as important to him as the acquisition and defence of territory was to mesolithic man. Con-cern about jobs is still concern about eating and breeding and the

★ These earlier 'layers' are discussed in the first part of the lecture, not re-printed here.

anxiety about losing the ability to make a living is very powerful. By that I mean that someone who has no fear of losing his job is naturally less concerned to make certain he retains it. Therefore the people who are responsible for creating employment approach the problem from an entirely different angle from the people who are seeking work or who are in danger of losing a job. Cold facts and reasoned argument may therefore entirely fail to convince.

Making a living is not solely dependent on having a job. There are many people who directly control the living they earn by their competence in commerce, in industry, or in a profession. In their case the dominant factor is not retaining a job but increasing the scope of their earning ability or in some cases expanding their reputation or making some useful contribution to human society. In spite of the fact that in these people the second and third layers are much thicker, the first layer is still there and probably finds expression in relation to their work or their homes, or to their attachment to the conventions of their group.

Although the primitive rules of behaviour have been more or less modified in individuals, the rules which govern group behaviour have changed rather less. What has changed almost beyond recognition is the environment in which groups of human beings operate. Territorial loyalty is very strong in nations, cities, provinces and villages. Group loyalty is very strong, for instance, in regiments, trade unions, professional groups, companies, clubs and all kinds of team sports. Provided the interests of different groups do not clash, people are quite capable of giving their loyalty to several different groups.

In fact one of the outcomes of our changing environment has been the multiplication of specialist groups. The State is losing its dominance as the group which commands general loyalty; instead international industrial corporations, trade unions, professional organisations, political parties and even age groups are gaining the individual's principal allegiance. Much of this is due to a feeling of weakness and uncertainty in the face of a blanketing bureaucracy. The case of doctors illustrates the point very well. Whereas they used to form an important part of the local group with whom they worked, they have now been forced to combine together in their own group. This combination and recombination of individuals for protection or for particular aspects of self-interest is causing a fragmentation of purpose within the larger group, the nation state.

Indeed this is also true on a wider scale. Reason suggests that the world needs greater centralised control through some form of world government, but in practice there is growing fragmentation. In certain situations loyalty to a group is both necessary and valuable but everyone has heard the expression: 'My country right or wrong'. This unquestioning loyalty can also be given to many other groups or ideologies and this causes a further erosion of reason. In the end the group or the ideology and its traditions begin to dominate its members and the greater the pressure on the group to change or modify its views, the more determined and unyielding its members become.

This group loyalty is reinforced by the natural tendency to conform to the conventions in thought and action of the group in which people find themselves or to which they attach themselves. The strength of this tendency is perhaps best demonstrated by the degree of conformity which exists among those who wish to be unconventional.

This tendency to conform to convention can exert a very powerful influence on the behaviour of individuals. If a child grows up in a group whose conventions are based on strong moral principles, for instance, it will find it relatively difficult to become a criminal. On the other hand, a child which grows up within a group of habitual criminals, will find it almost impossible to resist the tendency to conform to the conventions of the group.

In modern human civilisation survival pure and simple is no longer the only criterion; today the motive for endeavour is the physical and intellectual condition in which human populations exist. Territory continues to play a part, but many other things produce the same emotions. Vested interest, sporting, economic or cultural nationalism, are really only other names for the protection of group or individual territory.

But whether we like it or not, the classic process of natural selection still applies. Human conditions depend upon the economic success of groups and nations and in this economic competition it is the relatively more successful groups which are selected: the others wither and die. There may be many particular reasons for success or failure in this competition but all other factors being reasonably equal, it is still the organisation, together with the discipline and confidence – or the morale – of the human beings involved which will influence their behaviour and make the greatest contribution to the success of the group or nation.

Unlike the process of natural selection in the animal world, unsuccessful national economic systems can be changed by deliberate effort. For some reason, which I don't pretend to understand, we are quite capable of recognising the better results achieved by other systems, such as in Germany, the United States or Japan, but we do not seem capable of making an objective comparison of the theory and practice of the tax and administrative structures which have made these better results possible.

In fact the crux of the modern human problem is to achieve an organisation in government as well as in industry, commerce and the defence services, which allows the human beings involved to co-operate with the greatest efficiency and with the least friction. This can only be done by devising a compromise between primitive human demands and a rational administrative structure. This is important because whereas policy can be decided by detached, intelligent thought, the execution of that policy can only be effective if the human organisation allows. There is little value in devising intelligent policies or arriving at sensible decisions if the administrative organisation is unable to put either into execution.

Man's power of articulate reasoning has been the greatest influence in the development of our present civilisation. Therefore I believe that any further progress can only be made by more and better thought. Here we are up against a peculiar difficulty. The ordinary forces of natural selection have produced immensely complicated living structures and behaviour mechanisms. A great many are entirely automatic in the sense that there is no need to teach a mother how to develop an embryo, just as there is no need to train the larva of a Capricorn beetle.

The French entomologist Fabre studied this creature with great care and discovered that for three years the larva burrows about inside an oak tree, taking in wood at one end and leaving a tunnel behind. When the time comes for the larva to pupate it makes for the bark of the tree because the beetle could not exist in the ordinary wood. The larva then proceeds to hollow out a chamber just inside the wood, but close to the bark, big enough for the beetle which does not yet exist. It covers the walls and floor of the chamber with soft wood down, seals the openings and finally lies down with its head towards the exit. Were it to lie down the wrong way, the beetle would not be able to turn round to get out. I suspect that it would require training up to degree standard for a larva with the mental capacity of a man to get the whole process right by deliberate effort.

However, in that part of our civilisation brought about by human reasoning, virtually nothing is inherited. Children grow up physically with little difficulty, and they are capable of thought, but as far as the rational processes of the brain are concerned they begin totally ignorant. The whole basis of our existence has to be deliberately implanted: ideas and standards of behaviour, which experience and reason have found to be desirable, need to be transmitted before any new generation can play a full part in our present civilisation, let alone make any significant contribution to its further progress. I sometimes feel that, like the human embryo which seems to go through all the stages of the physical evolution of the species, the human child has to go through all the stages of our behavioural evolution.

Seen in the light, I believe that there is a good case for reviewing the whole structure and content of our educational process. Not perhaps on the purely scientific or academic side, although much could be done in the use of modern techniques of communication, but on that side which is concerned with the preparation of the next generation for the conditions of our existence as we are able to understand them today. For instance, it might be found that integration into responsible adult life at an earlier stage might make things a good deal easier for those who need to undergo a long period of education and training. It would also seem particularly necessary to help students to understand and to appreciate the origin of their natural instincts and emotions, and the way they have been modified over the ages. Not so that they can be warped or destroyed but so that the best can be encouraged and those which are less suitable for our civilised existence can be kept under control.

The conflict between instinct and reason has reached a critical stage in man's affairs, largely because the explosion of facts has revealed the instincts for what they are and at the same time it has undermined traditional philosophies and ideologies. The explosion of facts has effectively altered mankind's physical and intellectual environment and when any environment changes, the process of natural selection is brutal and merciless. 'Adapt or die' is as true today as it was at the beginning.

If we are to adjust to the new environment we must first of all accept that it exists and our whole approach to all our problems must be thoroughly realistic and based on discovered facts. We really cannot go towards the future facing backwards.

Now that we are beginning to understand the facts about the origins of our instincts and behaviour patterns, and are not just guessing at them, we should be in a much better position to devise human organisations which are at least compatible with them.

With our present knowledge and understanding we should be able to create more satisfactory national administrative organisations; more satisfactory for the people involved and more efficient as an organisation. We should be able to create more successful management systems, and better structures to take care of industrial relations. We should be able to so arrange our economic environment that there is a community of interest between all groups and individuals within the nation and a greater sense of common purpose.

After all, it is not the ability to manufacture and distribute soap powder, or the speed of modern transport, or the ability to reach the moon that matters. These are technical problems which can be solved by intelligent thought. What matters is that man should improve his control over his environment and his relationships so that, both as an individual and in his groups, he may be able to make a living in peace and in partnership with all his fellow creatures. Power determines our standards of living but intellect decides our standard of life.

The encouraging thing about man's evolutionary history is that in spite of set-backs, in spite of some dreadful aberrations of behaviour, the general trend has been for the better. Physical conditions are better for many and could be better for many more, while the evolution of thought has produced an intellectual environment vastly superior to that enjoyed by cave-men.

The trend is towards improvement, as it always has been, but we have now reached the stage where man has got to make a much greater conscious effort on behalf of the world as a whole.

If we use the mental capacities that we possess, with reason and with the knowledge at our command, there is no doubt whatever that we could lay the foundations for the next and most satisfactory period of man's long history.

from the Fawley Foundation Lecture, University of Southampton
SOUTHAMPTON, 24 NOVEMBER 1967

Prospects for Conservation

For hundreds of thousands of years people have been living in a more or less hostile environment. It was a constant struggle against what seemed to be the blind forces of nature. The greatest successes and achievements of mankind barely made any impression. Today all that is changed. We have got to get used to the idea that mankind is now dominant. It may have come as a great surprise, it may have been quite unintentional, but the fact remains that there is hardly a remote corner of this earth which is not subject to man's interference or control. Deep freezing, air-conditioning and modern transport, refuse collection and sewage disposal, have made life easier and removed it from the influence of climate and season. Synthetic materials and spare-part surgery have made us independent of nature and God.

This may sound rather arrogant, it may suggest that God's power has somehow been limited. This is not arrogance, this is realism. Industrial development, increasing population, pollution, exploitation of natural resources; these are the work of men. The power of God is still needed to influence mankind and to give direction to his activities, but it is no use behaving like spoilt children and blaming others when something goes wrong. We simply must get this straight: we are responsible for the things we do, we are responsible for the direct results of our actions and we must also take the blame for any indirect results.

At one time we could plead ignorance. When industrial methods began to be used on a large scale for the first time there were few, if any precedents and people did things which we now know to have been wrong and destructive. Today we ought to know that any ill-considered action may easily have disastrous results, not because of some outside malevolent influence but due entirely to our decisions.

At one time it seemed that the only hope of keeping the human species from extermination was to breed as many children as possible. Today the wastage through premature death and disease has been so much reduced that the same level of breeding is producing a population explosion. Whatever may be the moral arguments the fact remains that the total number of human inhabitants of this earth is growing at a truly alarming rate.

As far as this country is concerned a population of seventy million at the end of the century is going to mean a radical change in the physical aspects of these islands as we know them today. The direct result of this increase in the population is more space taken up by housing and these houses have got to be serviced by roads, sewage and refuse disposal, water and power supplies and with facilities for recreation and amenities. Furthermore these services will have to be supplied at a considerably higher standard than they are at present.

The indirect result of this increase in the population and the improved standards which will be provided is that industry must expand, and agriculture must become more efficient. There will have to be bigger industrial areas, more power stations, more transport, more reclamation of marginal land, more water supply and the whole operation will be conducted under the relentless pressure of competition. This competition will inevitably demand, as well as justify, scientific, technological and industrial innovation and the long-term influence of any innovation is bound to be a matter of speculation. This is the scene, this is the background to the whole problem of conservation facing us today.

Set against these purely practical considerations are the whole range of emotional, nostalgic and aesthetic feelings and attitudes towards the country we live in. All the things which bring richness and satisfaction to human existence. Everything which enlarges the quality of life. There is no doubt about it, people like old and historic buildings and constructions; people like the sweep and pattern of the countryside in the changing moods of the weather; there may be no rational explanation but people like the comradeship of their fellow creatures in the animal world, not as captive exhibits but as joint inheritors of the earth.

Conservation therefore means the process of reconciliation between the things which are needed for the practical satisfaction of people and those things which make life worthwhile.

Conservation means the care and protection of the historically interesting; it means the preservation of the naturally beautiful; and it means the considerate control and encouragement of wildlife.

This interpretation of the responsibilities of conservation can be further subdivided. We of the present generation living in this country at this particular moment in time have inherited a certain state of affairs, an environment created by circumstances of history and by contributions of all preceding generations together with certain things which we have done ourselves. We can either accept this state of things as inevitable and immutable or we can take a long cool look at them and come to some rational conclusion about them.

We have only to apply the very simple standards of cleanliness and tidiness to city and countryside to expose the immense potential for improvement. Even the most discouraging environment can be dramatically improved if it is well cared for. Every bit of every city is lived in by people. This experience can be much more pleasant if we take the trouble to see that the place looks nice, that it is clean and tidy, that there are suitable parks and gardens and that there are reasonable facilities for near-home recreation. Very little of the countryside goes unobserved so there is equally little reason to tolerate ugliness, decay, dereliction and neglect.

The first thing therefore is to care for the present environment, the next step is to care about the future. I don't pretend to be able to forecast what is going to happen, the future has always been full of surprises ever since man discovered how to think about it. However this world has been going for quite a long time and barring accidents it may well go on for quite a long time. So far one generation has succeeded another and again, barring accidents, there is every reason to believe that this process will continue. Something totally different may well happen but going entirely on past experience I think it would be reasonable to conclude that a hundred years from now this country will be inhabited by people not substantially different from ourselves. Many things about them may be different but broadly speaking it would be reasonable to guess that they too will enjoy the best achievements of previous generations, natural loveliness and the companionship of wild creatures.

If this is the case then the best we can do is to draw up plans so that they get what we believe they will enjoy. In fact the most important responsibility of conservation is planning. The plans may well be wrong but at least we will have tried, which is far better than leaving things to chance. Practically everything we enjoy today in our own environment was quite deliberately planned by previous generations, almost everything we deplore happened by chance or neglect.

This is an oversimplification, but I think it would be fair to say that for every slag heap which disfigures the countryside there must be ten parks or gardens deliberately created by people concerned about beauty.

This concern for beauty is as great, if not greater, today and the purpose of conservation is to mobilise this concern; to extend it from an individual attitude to a group consciousness; to create a wide public involvement so that each generation grows up aware of its responsibilities and so that public opinion is informed and active in all aspects of conservation.

Conservation is not simply a matter of preservation or an active concern for beauty. It must also take into account all the other activities which take place, particularly in the open country. It is concerned with sports and games and recreation in general; it is concerned with the use of water for all purposes; it is concerned with the use of land for agriculture and forestry and it is concerned with amateur and scientific study of wild animals and plants.

The reconciliation of all these conflicting interests in plans for the future is an immensely complicated and challenging task.

It demands co-operation and consultation between a great many bodies and organisations and it also demands from the Government an administrative structure capable of exercising the growing power of Parliament over all aspects of conservation and planning.

The fastest and most efficient railway engine cannot suddenly be taken on to a main road; for one thing it cannot be steered. In much the same way, an administrative structure admirably conceived long before conservation became vitally important is not in the best position to tackle the wholly new and strange problems thrown up by this new and increasingly widespread concern for our natural as well as our man-made surroundings.

Whatever may be done by the statutory authorities, it will never displace the need for active and enthusiastic voluntary organisations. If these organisations are to be fully effective they will have to create and maintain a sensible system of co-operation and a habit of working together. So many interests are involved and there are so many conflicting claims that the solution to every problem is bound to be a compromise and no one has yet discovered how to achieve a reasonable compromise without discussion and without mutual trust.

The first thing to do therefore is to find out, to become well informed, to master the facts. I can predict this with complete confidence: the more you learn about the problems of conservation the more concerned you will become, and it will need the concern of many people to stimulate the effective action which alone can make conservation a reality.

National Federation of Women's Institutes Conference
LONDON, 18 JULY 1968

Survival and Social Change

I suppose every generation has had to face daunting and unfamiliar situations but I wonder if any previous generation has had the feeling that it was riding a runaway roller-coaster and that things were happening almost too quickly to allow reasoned response or adequate control.

At least it can be said that if there is anything even remotely certain about this confused world, it is that every effect has a discoverable cause. The physical shape and activities of all living things, for instance, were caused by what has come to be known as natural selection. Every social convention in every population, from the most primitive to the most developed, has some practical origin. Every philosophical concept is the product of some human mind.

Inevitably this is reflected in the questioning of the established methods and ideas devised to control events and in the critical review of so-called traditional values and moralities.

I don't think this is very new; changes have been taking place ever since the dawn of history and every generation sees a new direction given to the development of human society. Change comes in two ways; there are conceptual changes – new ideas, new theories, changed priorities, different values; and there are material changes – new gadgets, new inventions, new factual knowledge, new applications of science and technology.

I realise that it is madly fashionable to get worked up about a new gadget or a new medicine as evidence of the brilliance of human progress but it's just as well to keep this sort of thing in perspective. Gadgets don't make civilisations. In fact they are just as likely to lead to a mechanised barbarism.

Up until about 150 years ago the rate of material change had been relatively slow compared to human intellectual development. Since that date material change has been taking place at an exponential rate. This is a new situation in human experience and I suspect that it is the cause of much of our present uncertainty.

If you look at things more carefully you will notice that all the most dramatic and fundamental changes in the human material environment took place between 150 and about 50 years ago. Mechanical devices for transport and manufacture had taken over almost completely from horses and handwork by the end of the First War. Electricity and electronics had taken over from candles, gas and steampower by a little later and ultimately they gave rise to telephones, radio and television.

Many of these changes have taken place within living memory. There are people alive today who remember the days before flight, before the motor car came into general use and before television began to exercise its power of mass hypnosis. Equally, a whole generation has grown up knowing nothing else. This sort of division of experience will never happen again on quite this scale.

Material change today is a matter of application and improvement, the period of radical change is over. There is a greater difference between flying and not flying than between flying and travelling to the moon. There is a greater difference between no radio and a crystal set than there is between radio and television. There is a greater difference between sail- and steam-driven ships than there is between steam- and nuclear-powered ships.

As far as material changes are concerned, all we are seeing today are variations, modifications and improvements upon methods, techniques and gadgets which were completely revolutionary about one hundred years ago. However, we are also witnessing something rather more serious. We are beginning to recognise some of the disturbing consequences of these triumphs of science and technology.

Indeed we are also beginning to foresee some of the consequences of indiscriminate progress. A good example is the development of computers and what might be called intelligent machines. Estimates of the effect they are going to have on human existence vary from horror to hope. I dare say they can be made to do almost anything; the question is what they ought to be made to do, provided always we retain control long enough to make such a decision.

Taking place at roughly the same time as this technological revolution was an eruption of knowledge. The trickle of scientific discovery very soon became a flood and when this flood reached down to the classrooms it produced an information explosion which effectively changed the whole background to human ideas and conceptions. As if that wasn't enough, the same period saw the immense development of the means of mass communication, informative, entertaining and commercial. It would be more than surprising if the attitudes and motives of this vast new estate did not influence the outlook and moralities of each new generation.

But it is the growing knowledge of facts which has given mankind the power to do virtually what he likes with the earth; we can exploit it, pollute it, and over-populate it if we so wish, but we can also deliberately prevent these things from happening. We can do this because we have the knowledge and the power. This new human power is so dazzling that to many people it has all the mystical attraction of one of the old religions. For those who either can't or don't want to think it is obviously very comforting to feel that everything can safely be left to science.

The great void of human factual knowledge used to be filled by God and as discovery followed discovery, so the dominating presence of God as an explanation began to recede. The first great questioning had begun and God was apparently replaced by scientific fact and rational explanation. I say 'apparently' because although God was once the great explanation He also had a completely different significance in relation to human behaviour which has so far not been satisfactorily superseded.

It would therefore be more than strange if this new power had not touched off a whole chain of consequent reactions. Not least has been the population explosion as a result of lifting the twin barriers of disease and starvation.

This is perhaps one rather obvious reaction; but less obvious is the effect which this material revolution has had upon conceptual development. The gradual emergence of liberal and egalitarian principles together with practical techniques in democratic government and the rule of law, took place against a relatively static material background. In the end a system existed which was not wholly unsuccessful even if it had a few glaring blemishes. It is these intellectual structures which are being questioned today for the simple reason that the background has changed faster than these structures have been able to adapt.

The system of central and local government, the law, the church, the universities and indeed our whole moral code, are all suddenly seen to have extraordinary and glaring inconsistencies with modern life. To some these inconsistencies mean that the whole structure is rotten and past repair, while to others the structures have become ends in themselves and therefore any modification must be resisted at all costs. Yet again to others it appears that the intellectual principles on which the structures were founded are still perfectly sound and valid and the only problem is to adapt the methods and techniques to the modern situation.

I am, perhaps naturally, inclined to the view that the principles are still valid even if the practice is creaking a bit under the strain. I believe this largely because I doubt if any one age or generation has a monopoly of all the wisdom and all the virtues. I suspect that some of our predecessors were not as silly as some seem to imagine and that we could do worse than accept conclusions which have been hammered out over a long period of time.

On the other hand the most challenging proposition is the first because if all these structures are beyond modification or repair it means that something entirely new and original must be put in their places. Anyone who advocates the abolition of all existing structures and fails to suggest a better or even an alternative solution is not really worth bothering about. I dare say you have all noticed that small children display great talent in knocking down a tower of building blocks without showing any inclination or ability to build one.

To understand how mankind arrived at the situation where his affairs are controlled by religion, convention and law you have to go back a bit.

Circumstances entirely beyond human control decreed that out of the animal world should evolve a type of primitive man, probably closely related in habits and social structure to other forms of anthropoid ape. Evolutionary pressure was intense and at some point primitive man developed the use of weapons or tools and in so doing gave an advantage to those of his breed who were most successful at co-ordinating hand and eye and brain.

In due course grunts gave way to more precise communication and from that moment man stepped into a wholly new and separate class of evolution from the rest of the animal world. His physical and behavioural evolution advanced as slowly as ever but at this moment he started on the entirely new and much more exciting course of intellectual evolution.

Speech gave him a tremendous practical advantage over all other animals but it also made it possible to discuss things, to pass on useful information, to instruct, to co-operate and above all to ask the question 'why?'. I suppose it was entirely inevitable that sooner or later someone would come up with an answer, which although not strictly accurate, at least could not be disproved at the time, particularly if it appeared to have some sort of supernatural sanction.

Every now and then one group or other of unrelated human populations made some spectacular advance either in ideals of government, in social behaviour, in philosophical concepts or in the development of abstract capacities such as mathematics and astrology.

However, constantly lurking behind this intellectual development was the old Adam, full of deeply embedded behaviour patterns and instincts. Fear bred of the uncertainty of life, fear of the unknown and the strange, created hate of everything except the familiar. Fear also created affection as a means of self-preservation. A conscience is really only a reflection of do's and don'ts learned subconsciously at an impressionable age. The whole story of man is the endless struggle between a rational intellect and instinctive emotion, typified perhaps by the ideals of marriage and the temptations of adultery.

There have been many attempts to integrate these two factors but from our own European point of view the most successful and most influential was the teaching of Christ. I am not referring now to any religious or supernatural aspects but simply to what He is recorded to have said. He, and later St Paul, saw quite clearly the dreadful dichotomy in man's soul; they saw quite clearly that there was no future for man if he was ruled only by his passions.

It was Christ who formulated the concept that love was better than hate, that compassion was better than selfishness and tolerance better than prejudice. He also saw that fear was at the root of man's troubles and so he substituted a God of love and concern for the old God of fury and vengeance.

It so happened that at the time of Christ, religion, philosophy and politics were all very closely interwoven. It should be no surprise therefore that in our Western European civilisation, Christianity, religion and morals came to be almost synonymous.

Of course it is perfectly true that vast numbers of people came to join what they looked upon as the Christian religion, but continued to live and behave like savages, accepting the ceremonial, but letting their natures be governed entirely by their passions.

It is true that history is full of the most dreadful horrors perpetrated in the name of religion. It is true that systems of government and law based on Christian ethics have condoned injustice, intolerance and prejudice. This is all true, but this does not mean that the idea has no merit, it merely emphasises the difficulty of imposing a sufficient restraint upon human nature. Perhaps we have simply failed to find the best way to condition people to the standards of a better civilisation.

If you set about removing the structures which are based, however imperfectly, upon these, in our case, Christian principles, you don't just wipe the slate clean. You don't, as Rousseau would have it, release or rediscover the noble savage. You revert from a deliberate and rational restraint on human emotion to the instinctive behaviour patterns which have been lurking just below the surface all the time. You don't even remove the instinct for religious ceremonial or the cult of the supernatural, it is merely transferred from one system of ethics to another.

This is not wild speculation, as you will very soon discover if you take a look at the mode of existence of those human groups which either abandoned or never had any system of social restraints, and compare it with the behaviour of our nearest collateral relations in the animal world.

Indeed this sort of human community is capable of atrocities far worse than any animal population would even dream about. Even when the restraints come off only temporarily, almost anything can happen. Six million Jews were killed during the last war and one night-bombing raid on Dresden killed over 130,000 people.

Material conditions have changed beyond all recognition and this has created a new intellectual situation. We now have a whole new set of fears and anxieties and even the old anxieties have changed in scale and priority. It is therefore only natural to want to be released from conventional restrictions which were adopted to meet a situation which no longer exists, but removing one lot of restraints – even if they are not always effective – without considering if others might be necessary, can only lead to difficulties.

Where some of these conventional restrictions are being questioned or ignored it has come to be known as permissiveness, and so long as this applies to those restrictions which are no longer relevant there can be little argument. However indiscriminate permissiveness cuts both ways; if it allows this why not allow that? If it is based entirely on self-interest it would surely result in materialism run wild.

The sole criterion for any action would be whether something could be done, whereas morality has to do with whether something ought to be done. This doesn't end with personal and individual problems. Science and technology have advanced to such a point that virtually anything can be done, so much so that governments are facing increasingly difficult decisions about what should be done and how it should be done. Birth control, abortion, euthanasia and priorities in medicine and the social services are obvious examples. In systems where government is by discussion, these decisions will be influenced by individual ethics.

Some might argue that experience and any form of conventional morality are unimportant because there is a natural law of right and wrong and the criterion is human fulfilment. This is altogether too naive. In this context the only natural laws are survival, aggression and revenge, and if we cannot find comprehensive inhibitions or positive motivations the struggle becomes totally unscrupulous.

In any case if there are relaxations in some of our conventional restrictions these are more than compensated for in the immense growth of institutional restrictions. The tremendous increase in central and local legislation, the complication of tax laws and the vast bureaucracy needed to manage them can hardly be labelled as giving greater liberty to the individual. After all liberty means the ability to exercise choice and choice is the one thing which legislation restricts. These restrictions may be in the interest of a fair distribution of wealth and for other social purposes, but they are still restrictions. Why not take permission to break these restrictions?

This then appears to be the nub of the problem, because it doesn't need much reflection to realise that an immensely complicated material environment cannot be controlled or improved by the law of the jungle. Things are bad enough as they are and if that thin veneer of rational morality and agreed social disciplines is removed, they won't get any better.

The process of questioning which is getting so much attention is very proper and reasonable, provided always that it is for the purpose of discovery, and not simply an excuse to condemn structures and attitudes from a position of bias or ignorance. This merely confounds prejudice with more prejudice.

There are of course a great many questions of detail which need to be asked all the time but I think the central issue is this: man has acquired an immense factual knowledge about physical existence and this knowledge has enabled him to populate the earth in what amounts to plague proportions, it has enabled him to create an immensely complicated material environment, it has put in his hands destructive powers of staggering proportions, it has in fact given him virtually complete control over his habitat.

We can, of course, ignore the opportunity to exercise this control and just leave things to chance. On the other hand we are in the position of being able to exercise this control consciously and deliberately. This is a colossal responsibility and the difficulty is to decide just how this control is to be exercised. This brings us back full circle to the first questions ever asked, 'What am I doing here? What is the purpose of life?'

Those may be the ultimate questions and I dare say we shall go on asking them for a very long time. In the meanwhile history and experience seem to indicate that even if we don't know the purpose of it all, we do at least know quite a lot about how the world works and that barring accidents it will go on working for quite some time into the future. In this sense knowledge is responsibility.

Accepting responsibility means accepting the need to make a choice and to take a decision. In the same way that you cannot get a solution to even the simplest problem from a computer before you devise and insert the programme, so it is impossible for us to take any kind of decision without some knowledge of the facts and some broad guidelines of principle.

It is all very well to point to what appear to be obvious cases such as concern for welfare of the very young, the sick and the very old, but even this concern must be based on some generally accepted view of human existence. It must be a generally accepted view so that both the doers of good and the receivers of service recognise the same motive.

At one time these guidelines were established by Christian principles, and decisions were taken based upon the facts as they were known and upon an interpretation of God's will and purpose. Indeed many orders of Christian monks and nuns and many hospital and charitable foundations were based directly on the

Christian concept of concern for others. Their work was not looked upon as patronising because everyone recognised the motives on which it was based. If those motives are rejected then some other form of guidelines must be found and they must command the same degree of popular support.

I think it is fairly certain that without some acceptable alternative motive, the old laws of survival will reassert their authority. Fear and hate will once again dominate decisions and authority will be exerted by the biggest and strongest gang, aided and abetted by all the techniques of public relations. We shall come face to face with the same dilemma which has haunted mankind since he learned to think; how to exert some rational control over the brute forces of natural selection, how to substitute a system based on thought and reflection for a system dictated by the competitive pressure of survival.

All the great human civilisations can trace their success to some generally accepted system of control and restraint. Some were based on authority derived from a supernatural source, others derived their strength from a system of shared authority and general participation. Where such a system failed to develop communities remained in a barbarous and primitive state. Where the system decayed or was overthrown the civilisation gradually collapsed and disintegrated.

Today it is absolutely certain that material development by itself cannot sustain our civilisation. To make life tolerable and indeed possible for intelligent man there must be some criterion of right and wrong, some positive motivation, some vision of an ideal, some beckoning inspiration. Without it we shall never get to grips with the population explosion and racial prejudice, with starvation, and the distribution of resources; with the conflicting demands of development and conservation, of progress and pollution, or the control of complex industrial communities and the liberty of the individual.

Devising a new system or even revising what remains of the existing system is a fairly daunting prospect. It has to take into account everything we know about the universe and the earth's situation within it, about the earth itself and our relationship to it; about ourselves and our relationship to each other, and about our existing industrial, commercial, legal and political structures. From this it must distil a theory which commands such a degree of acceptance that people will find the will to make it work, recognising the need for the restraints which it demands and the responsibilities and obligations which it imposes.

A new system might well be devised which satisfied the rational and impersonal judgement of scientists or economists or even students, but that isn't enough. There is a wide gap between group toleration and private conviction. In the end the system has got to satisfy the individual throughout his life and in all circumstances. It must provide him with some sort of moral criterion. It must provide him with some reference point to help him decide between right and wrong and he must accept it with such conviction that it can sustain him through periods of crisis, adversity and depression.

I said the system has got to satisfy the individual because in our tradition the individual matters. Our whole legal system is designed to protect the individual, our political system is based on consensus of opinion and the voluntary acceptance of decisions. Under this system a community is composed of participating individuals and therefore the ideals and the convictions of individuals are all-important.

For instance the Christian Church may have a particular group philosophy but its concern is with individuals and if Christian philosophy finds its way into daily life, into economics and politics or into the law, or into any other structure, it is the result of the influence of convinced individuals and not the result of Church policy.

It may well be that the idea of the importance of the individual is no longer tenable in modern circumstances and that we need some other basic criterion. However, I doubt whether any system which demands a high degree of conformity and which stifles individual will and conscience can be satisfactory for very long. It may well be more efficient but its efficiency will be bought at the price of much human misery and frustration.

Successful organisms need a prime motivation and sense of

purpose but they must also contain a proportion of irrelevant features in their structure so that when change occurs one or other of these features may suddenly turn out to be essential to survival under the new conditions.

This means that for any human intellectual structure to survive, to adapt to changing conditions and to improve its civilised qualities, it must allow a certain freedom and a certain tolerance of conflicting views and ideas so that development can continue. The system cannot survive if it becomes too rigid; equally if the system becomes totally dominated by conflict, disagreement and stalemate, experience shows that disintegration follows rapidly.

I said at the start that I am a spectator of events and developments. Looking around at the moment it would not be very difficult for anyone to point out all the warts and blemishes of our system; it can be very amusing to seek out all the discreditable events in history and to make people feel embarrassed and ashamed.

The consequence is simple: people lose confidence, they lose the sense of purpose and motivation which is so essential to the maintenance of a measure of civilisation. My reflection leads me to conclude that we have to make a choice. We can either stick to our existing principles and adapt our structures and social disciplines to modern conditions, or we can try to create a new set of principles and structures. What we cannot do with any hope of improving our civilisation is to drift aimlessly, pulled this way and that by self-interest and expediency.

This, it seems to me, is what the questioning should be about. If we don't come to some conclusion about this question fairly soon, time will run out on us and we shall start sliding down the slippery slope which may not lead to chaos and confusion but will certainly lead to the end of our relatively free civilisation as we know it, and all our ideals of humanity, compassion and individual human dignity will disappear.

Oration, King's College, London
LONDON, 3 DECEMBER 1969

Doomwatchers and Cheermongers:
The Role of Industry and Commerce
in Conservation

I would imagine that every generation thinks of itself as unique in human history. But I believe it is possible to make out a very good case that the people who have lived during the last hundred years have experienced something rather exceptional. They have lived in and through the industrial, scientific and technological revolutions.

There are many people alive today who were born, if you come to think of it, before aircraft, before motor cars, radio, telephones, television or space exploration. Many indeed grew up without electric light or running water in their homes. Only the teenagers of today have lived all their lives under the new conditions and although we have not seen the end of technological development, I doubt whether the world will ever see such radical technical innovations ever again. The result of the revolutions is that a general standard of material existence in the advanced countries is such as no previous generation has ever enjoyed. Even in the less technically advanced areas there has been a dramatic improvement of health services, agricultural techniques and industrial development.

Up to now the concern has been with change, development, expansion and the exploitation of potential scientific knowledge and discovery. I believe we are slowly coming out of that phase. I believe there is quite a lot of evidence that we are entering a post-revolutionary phase when people start looking around to assess what has happened.

Concern for nature, worry about the exploitation of natural resources, anxiety about the rapidly increasing world population, a nagging dread about future world food production, a growing interest in all aspects of the human environment, living and housing conditions, pollution, noise, recreation and the future of cities in the motor car age; all these things point to a changing outlook. To many people the bandwagon of development and exploitation at any cost is no longer as attractive as it used to be. The new bandwagon I suspect is an attempt to create a humanly acceptable way of life within this new materially prosperous framework. The next phase is going to be a very complicated process of picking up the bits of civilised human existence after the explosion of knowledge and technology and putting them together into a pattern which matches the new environment.

Now put like that it sounds reasonable and not too difficult. It is therefore not really very surprising, I suppose, that there are so many people with such an utter and implacable conviction that their particular solution is absolutely right, and that it is self-evident that the pattern of human existence they have in mind is the only one worth considering. I sometimes rather envy people who can be so completely convinced of their own infallibility. I am afraid I see the future as full of dilemmas and contradictions and I believe that many of these dilemmas are particularly relevant to the functions and responsibilities of industry and commerce.

Any objective and intelligent assessment of the future must take into account the predictable outcome of economic, technological and population growth at the present increasing rate, if it is not controlled. At the same time it is really not possible to deny training and education in just those disciplines and professions which thrive on, and encourage, yet more growth.

Furthermore, the current philosophy is that industrial creativity, originality and innovation are the desirable characteristics, but if the future depends upon arriving at some form of equilibrium then those characteristics will have to be modified or at least redirected. Conservation of resources, maintenance of existing plants, recycling of materials, greater economy in consumption, a more modest ambition for utopia; these will have to become the desirable attitudes, but I suspect that such a sudden reversal of philosophy would have some very difficult consequences.

It is only too obvious that the vastly improved material standards for a very wide section of the community are directly due to technological development and economic growth. Any restriction on growth could well be seen to be a restriction on the growth of economic prosperity for those who are less well off.

In spite of some very convincing evidence that there are absolute limits to world population growth, and to the world supply of currently useful non-renewable resources, and that these limits will be reached in the not so distant future, there are many people – reasonably or unreasonably – who feel that they would prefer the apparent certainty of being better off in the short term than worry about a theoretical possibility of a collapse in the slightly longer term.

Even the straightforward ambition to be better off raises problems. The vicious circle of costs, incomes and prices is a very topical subject just now, even though some commentators are blandly confident that all increases in costs and wages can be absorbed by higher productivity. It is beginning to look as if even greater productivity has its rational limits, particularly at a time of an increasing labour force. Increased leisure might provide part of the answer but when does leisure become under-employment?

Furthermore, there are expectations of higher standards of living but these really depend on better service industries, which find it difficult to match the higher wages available in the high-productivity manufacturing industries. In any case, no country can decide these things for itself if it is dependent on competition in world markets.

There is a very understandable concern for the conservation of the human environment, but how is this to be achieved against the need for essential development? In the next fifty years, in this country alone, we are going to have to create the equivalent of four new Birminghams. The physical and social problems alone are bad enough but finding gainful employment is going to be really serious.

We are concerned about the conservation of nature and wild-life, yet this is hardly compatible with present urban and industrial growth rates, and present agricultural developments, all of which demand a more intensive use of the available land.

We are concerned with human freedom, yet when we have got it there is always someone who will shamefully exploit it. Control and direction is the inevitable outcome. Every piece of legislative control, even if it is for the benefit of some people, is a restriction on the freedom of others. The problem, whether it is the in-dividual who matters or whether individuals shall only exist for the benefit of the state, has been debated for many years. At the present rate of progress, there will be no choice. Existence on the scale in prospect is only possible under the strictest control.

In recent years many more people have become alive to the side effects of unrestrained development. This change has caused some very deep tensions between conservationists and developers. The tensions are made worse by the fact that there are so many factors involved. In the first place, the conservation lobby is itself divided into those who are concerned with the effects of industrial and urban developments on the human environment. They are concerned with the social problems of big cities, recreation facilities, open spaces, clean air and clean beaches. The other division is concerned with the effect of industrial and urban development on the natural environment and with the human exploitation of wild populations. They are principally concerned with the protection of wildlife. In some cases the aims of the two groups are compatible but in many cases they are not. They are on common ground when it involves pollution of any kind but they are inclined to part company when it comes to the effect of herbicides and pesticides in agriculture. They can compromise when it comes to the conservation of wild game populations but the human environmentalists are less concerned about the com-mercial exploitation of wild populations, whether they are marine animals or in forest areas.

The two parties can agree about areas which should be

protected against industrial or urban development but while one group sees the area as a potential for human recreation, the other sees human recreation as just another disturbance of the wild populations.

The developers are also in a bit of a quandary. Most of them see the need to control pollution, for example, but unlike the conservationists they are a bit more conscious of the price factor. On the other hand, many of them are only conscious of their own particular area of activity and find it difficult to see the combined effect of a myriad of large and small developments of different kinds. They mainly believe in conservation in theory but they cannot be expected to pass up a good economic prospect without a struggle.

The Government is in an even worse quandary, as it is being pressed on all sides, with the developers pointing out the national need for resources and employment, the human environmentalists fighting for better conditions for people and the natural environ-mentalists hopefully trying to protect the wild populations.

Overhanging the whole problem like a smog are the doom-watchers and the cheermongers locked in deadly combat. One side prophesies ecological holocaust and destruction by pollution, and therefore preaches anti-growth and technophobia. On the other side, we have bland reassurance that everything is for the best and that the world is a self-righting system which will ensure that all the problems will be dealt with before a serious crisis arises.

As usual, I suspect the truth is somewhere between the two. I believe we are faced with problems on a scale which the world has never seen before, but I do not believe in inevitable doom. I am quite prepared to believe that the world is a self-righting system but I suspect that the process of self-righting is much too drastic to be allowed to happen. I believe that we have got to do the righting ourselves and I firmly believe that it can be done, now that so many people are beginning to understand the risks and dangers ahead.

The City of Westminster Chamber of Commerce
LONDON, 9 APRIL 1973

Dilemmas in Conservation

The word 'conservation' can be used in many connections but I am going to use it in the context of the conservation of the environment. By this I mean the creation of a satisfactory state of existence for all living things on this earth. It includes the protection of the best of what we have inherited, the correction of the worst mistakes, and the considerate planning of future development.

However, the word 'environment' can also be made to refer to all sorts of situations but for the purposes of this lecture I am only concerned with two. First, there is the human environment which is really a reflection of mankind's egocentric view of the world as his exclusive home and playground. This includes all aspects of culture, folklore and architecture. Secondly, there is the natural environment which is where all other living things attempt to exist, with the exception of those which have been domesticated.

I have made an assumption that it is, in fact, desirable to create a satisfactory state of existence for all living things. There is obviously no question about creating a satisfactory state of existence for *Homo sapiens* and those animals and plants which serve his needs, but the conservation of the other forms of life is rather a different issue. The problem arises because in the majority of cases involving the conservation of nature it is the needs of mankind which pose the greatest threat and, therefore, decisions have to be made between the claims of man and the claims of nature.

Inevitably the decisions are liable to go in favour of man because we are both the claimant as well as the judge, we make the rules of evidence, we call the witnesses and we have to pay the costs. This means that we have to establish good reasons for admitting that nature has some claims in its own right.

Many people feel that the pleasure and relaxation which undisturbed nature and wildlife give to mankind is sufficient reason for its conservation. But this is treating nature as if it was part of the human environment. It is an entirely self-centred argument.

Then there is the scientific argument that everything in nature is inter-related and the product of an immensely long process of development and evolution. Our whole world and everything on it and in it is, therefore, scientifically interesting. This makes the earth into a laboratory and all living things so many specimens. This point of view does at least suggest that nature has some claims to consideration and continued existence in its own right.

Then again there is what might be described as the religious argument. This says that everything was created by God and, therefore, each creation must have some value or it would not have been created. The fact that mankind has become the most powerful and influential of God's creatures merely means that it has a correspondingly greater responsibility for the welfare of its fellow creatures. This may strike some people as rather old-fashioned but again it gives nature a very definite claim to consideration.

Perhaps the most telling argument can only be put in the negative sense. Is it really conceivable that we should sit idly by either in ignorance, indifference or greed and simply allow one life form after another to disappear from the face of the earth? Furthermore, this is not a question for mankind in general, it is a question for our generation in particular because unless the decision to admit that nature has a genuine claim to continued existence is taken in our time, the pressures of human expansion will lead inevitably to an irreversible decline and ultimate elimination of wild populations.

In an effort to present the dilemmas caused by the desire to conserve nature in some coherent sequence I have arbitrarily divided them into categories:

(1) *Agriculture versus Nature*

This is probably the most awkward category because agriculture is a controlled natural process in itself and its activities have a direct bearing on the development of human material standards of living.

Agriculture has made immense demands on nature. I do not need to remind you of the figures of the increase in world population which by its sheer physical size occupies an ever-growing proportion of the earth's surface. I do not need to remind you that every mouth wants to be fed, therefore, the demand for the production of more food and the search for new resources of agricultural land is encroaching at an increasing rate on the so far natural and undisturbed areas which are the homelands of wild populations of animals and plants.

Clearing bush and draining marshes brings new land into production but it also destroys the habitats of wild animals or it drastically interferes with the natural food chains. The critical problem here is to make sure that certain species are not dispossessed altogether in the process and threatened with extinction as a result.

Once an area has been brought into agricultural production the machinery takes over and woe betide any animal which is bold enough to try to exist in an environment of ploughs, harrows, cutters, harvesters, sprayers, fertilisers and the burning of straw.

It is well known that certain chemical pesticides, herbicides and fungicides can make a significant contribution to productivity, but a great many of them are acknowledged to be very toxic to wildlife. A typical example is the locust plague which is affecting large areas in eastern Australia. The plague has to be controlled but it is not easy to balance the penalties against the advantages. There is a very real dilemma between the claims of food production for a hungry world and the survival of wild populations.

Another natural resource exploitation which creates a serious dilemma is forestry. Commercial planting and cropping of trees which are frequently of an exotic species, create particular problems. First, because if it is exotic it is unsuitable for indigenous species. Commercial forestry tends to be a monoculture with all the attendant risks of pest infestation, and also because the normal cycle of regeneration, maturity and decay is not allowed to take place. However, from the point of view of wild animal populations the clear felling of a natural stand of timber for conversion into woodchips for paper, board or cellulose manufacture is far more serious because the whole ecological structure disappears and only the hardiest and most adaptable species succeed in lingering on or in rare cases take advantage of the new conditions and so become a pest.

Not directly related to agriculture but involving the processes of nature is the provision of fresh water supplies to the growing demands of domestic and industrial consumers. The present system appears almost totally irrational. Water is abstracted before it gets into the rivers and is then stored in reservoirs which have to be taken from agricultural, common or even national park land. The water is used for industrial or domestic purposes, treated by the best technological means available and then pumped back into the rivers, in many cases with a sufficient proportion of dissolved nitrates to create the phenomenon known as eutrophication. It does not need much imagination to appreciate the damage this does to terrestrial and aquatic animals which exist in marshes, rivers and swamps. The only compensation is that those reservoirs which are not simply concrete-lined tanks do support a lot of wildlife.

(2) *Industry versus Nature*

Agriculture uses natural processes to produce food but industry depends on inert raw materials which it converts into capital and consumer goods. The impact of industry on nature is, therefore, quite different but the conflict with conservation is just as real.

It begins with the extraction of raw materials. Underground mining may not have a direct impact on nature but the processing activities on the surface are quite significant, particularly if they involve slag heaps, land subsidence and noxious effluents in the rivers. Opencast mining on the other hand has a very obvious impact on nature although modern methods of rehabilitation greatly reduce any lasting damage unless, of course, it destroys some rare ecological system or habitat.

The main influence of the manufacturing phase lies in the pollution caused by releasing noxious effluents into the air and into water courses or the sea. The problem with this is that any attempt to control these effluents adds an extra cost to manufacture which is inevitably passed on to the consumer. The problem is compounded if some countries apply stricter controls on effluents than others. The situation becomes quite ludicrous if authorities on opposite banks of an international waterway, or whose rivers drain into a restricted sea, apply different regulations. The efforts of a conservation-conscious authority on one side are then totally defeated by the profit-conscious authority on the other.

Having got through the manufacturing stage it may well happen that the product itself causes pollution or otherwise interferes with the natural environment. Motor cars are accused of the former and once any product becomes waste it interferes with the latter.

The impact of modern methods of transport as a whole on the natural environment causes immense problems. Roads, railways and airfields can all have directly devastating effects. Modern highways and motorways cut right through previously undisturbed areas and act as virtual barriers to the movement of wild animals. In Germany, for instance, it is suspected that hares have been almost wiped out by being killed on the roads.

Perhaps the most direct impact of industry on the environment lies in the disposal of worn-out products. The irony is that disposal is even more significant than the original extraction of the raw materials. Extraction creates a hole, disposal fills a hole but unfortunately not necessarily the same hole.

In principle, the useful materials from articles for disposal should be extracted and recirculated. However, this is a relatively expensive and awkward process which is unlikely to be generally adopted until the price of raw materials rises to equal the cost of recirculated materials. We shall then witness the edifying spectacle of waste tips being mined for rare and expensive raw materials and the long overdue construction of waste segregation and recirculation plants.

(3) *Human Pleasure and Leisure versus Nature*

Certain people like a natural wilderness and they will go to great lengths to get particular areas of natural beauty, scientific interest or particular forms of wildlife, protected from any kind of development or commercial exploitation. The difficulty here is that these national parks and reserves are hard to justify unless they allow human access for leisure and pleasure. The moment this happens they are no longer wilderness areas and while some animal populations, as in the great African parks, can accept this type of human penetration many other areas are much more vulnerable. One solution might be to allow only limited access but this is very difficult to achieve in practice as the areas are usually quite large without any physical barriers on their boundaries. We have not yet come to accept the idea that some areas should be kept either wholly or partially undisturbed by human activity for the direct benefit of wild populations.

The other area in which human pleasure conflicts with conservation is in the taking of wild animals for sport. Some species may be described as pests, some are a source of food, but there are others which need to have their numbers controlled if only to ensure that they do not destroy their artificially limited habitat. In the latter case, the problem lies in whether it is better to pay someone to do the killing or whether to accept the fact that amateurs can do it just as well. As far as the amateur is concerned he is obviously going to make sure that his quarry is not exterminated, while the professional is torn between making the best profit and doing himself out of a job if he succeeds too well.

The taking of game is a very old-established pursuit and in this country it involves the employment of gamekeepers. The function of these people is to see that game, and in most cases this means wild populations, can flourish. However, their dilemma is that in order to conserve the game species they are required to control the predator species and from the conservation of nature point of view this may well be very destructive. On the other hand the control of predators means that many more non-destructive birds can survive in greater numbers.

In many other countries the idea that game should belong to the land holder or that rights to take game should be let by the owner is considered to be very undemocratic. Game is wild, therefore it is God's gift to every man. This system either results in the disappearance of all animals or in a bag limit for each species of game. The difficulty is that as more people go out after the game the bag limit has to be reduced until it is so small that cheating is inevitable. Strangely enough the control of game is far stricter in most Communist countries than it is in several European countries.

Man is certainly the most effective predator the world has ever known, but not always as a killer. A most important clash between pleasure and conservation occurs in egg collecting. Collecting is a compulsive habit and unfortunately the more rare a particular specimen may be the more it is valued. So much so that some people find it possible to make a living by collecting and selling the eggs of rare species. Even the famous osprey's nest at the Boat of Garten has not been spared.

Similar to egg collecting is specimen collecting. This applies to research workers and particularly to big game. Under controlled conditions this does no harm, but the indiscriminate taking of specimens from wild populations whose statistics are not properly understood is quite indefensible.

Much the same applies to big game fishing, but particularly to underwater spear-gun fishing or lobster catching which is not at all easy to control and which can pluck an area absolutely clean in a very short time. The pernicious point about any free-for-all system is that even quite responsible people will take what they can because they know that if they do not get it someone else surely will. Perhaps the most satisfactory solution to the problem of the free-for-all situation is by mandatory membership of a club or association with exclusive rights in particular areas.

There is a different form of specimen collection which involves the capture of wild animals for display in zoos and for commercial exploitation in the so-called safari parks. It is unfortunately inevitable that the rarer the species the more desirable it is. However, I am glad to say that most of the zoos of the world have come to recognise the dangers and their own responsibilities. The taking of rare wild animals is discouraged while at the same time the zoos have been making great efforts to encourage the breeding of rare species already in captivity.

(4) *Human Need versus Human Pleasure*

This does not appear to involve nature at all and in most cases there is no particular threat to a rare species involved. On the other hand it represents a real dilemma in that it requires someone to make a choice for or against some form of development. Perhaps the most famous and intractable example is the case of Lake Pedder in south-west Tasmania.

The lake lies in an area which until recently was almost impenetrable and which had been declared a reserve. The gist of the problem is that the Hydro Electric Commission designed a very ambitious scheme which involved building a dam and creating a vast storage reservoir. Unfortunately Lake Pedder was included in the reservoir area which meant that the original lake was to be flooded under an extra thirty feet of water. Biologists pointed out that certain insects and plants were unique to the peculiar beach structure of the original lake and were liable to be exterminated, but it is much more difficult to stir up emotion about an insect than some appealing furry animal or spectacular bird. The main objection therefore is that the development has seriously modified an area of untouched natural beauty.

Fundamentally, this is a clash between the human desire to preserve a certain area in an undisturbed form on the one hand and the determination to harness natural resources to human needs on the other.

(5) *Conservation versus Nature*

This may sound like a contradiction but the problem arises simply because it is no longer possible to ensure large enough undisturbed areas in which the natural balances of nature can operate satisfactorily in keeping the various wild populations under control.

A very typical example is the Tsavo National Park in East Africa where natural and human predation of the elephant stock was suddenly stopped with the result that the elephants suffered a population explosion and were well on their way to changing the whole ecology of the Park. It was, therefore, proposed that the population should be controlled by cropping, but this was not universally acceptable for a number of reasons. In the end the problem was solved by a very severe drought which drastically reduced the number of elephants in the Park.

Altogether the control of pests whether by shooting, trapping, poisoning or artificially induced disease or sterility and predation is a very difficult issue. In most cases pests are simply wild populations which we do not like for one reason or another and it is a strange quirk of human morality that while some object to the killing of some animals and many abhor the use of so-called inhumane methods of killing others, no one seems to mind how pests are controlled. Furthermore, there is an entirely irrational concern based on the size or the appeal of the animal. The rule is that the smaller or the uglier the animal the less concern about its fate.

Inevitably, the conservationist is most concerned with those species which are in danger of extinction and with their habitats, but what no one knows for certain is whether the species would be dying out from natural causes or whether it is due to human interference.

Perhaps the most difficult problem is to decide to what extent conservation measures are themselves interfering with the process of evolution and natural selection. A wild population will have evolved to its present state as a result of the conditions and pressures under which it has tried to exist. If those pressures are suddenly removed or changed the selection of those strains which are most suitable for the conditions is also changed and it is quite possible to lose important characteristics within a relatively few generations.

(6) *Money versus Nature*

Failing a moral argument for or against conservation the economic argument is always decisive. The assessment of any industrial or technical development project is based on a cost benefit analysis.

If the economic benefits can be shown to be greater than the economic costs the plan goes ahead. The dilemma for the conservationist is to quantify the cost to the natural or to the human environment in economic terms so that it can be compared with the figures of the economic benefits. This is of course very unfair because it simply is not possible to quantify the value of nature.

However, it might also be possible to stand the problem on its head. Perhaps it might be possible to use the conservation criterion rather than money in the cost benefit analysis. In other words, instead of trying to make conservation justify its case in money terms, it might be an idea to make the developer justify his case in conservation terms.

(7) *The Dilemma of Conservation Organisation*

The first dilemma is to find a generally acceptable reason for conservation which is not entirely based on the pleasure, convenience and economic demands of the human population. Without that it is very difficult to put a case which is not suspected of being due to prejudice, emotion, sheer crankiness or self-interest.

Then there is the recurring dilemma between control and preservation. There is a very strong body of opinion, mostly I suspect of urban origin, which is against the killing of animals for any reason, except domestic animals as a source of food. It is almost impossible to establish the idea that there is a very great difference between killing individual animals on the one hand and exterminating a whole species by not allowing it anywhere to exist on the other. It is equally difficult to establish that conservation also involves keeping wild populations down to a number suitable to the habitat which is available for it.

By far the most difficult problem for conservation bodies is to decide how to put their case. Some believe in persuasion and compromise and the use of legal and legislative methods to achieve their ends. Others find this approach does not get the results they hope for. In consequence, they are driven to confrontation and outright opposition by all possible means. This can achieve results but it has its dangers because it can lead to personal abuse and even violence.

It so happens that mankind has become by far the most powerful of all the living things and my belief is that we, therefore, have a clear responsibility for all life on this planet. We know only too well what happens when men acquire power without a sense of responsibility. I am convinced that it would be a major disaster for all future generations of mankind if we, who are alive at this critical point in history, were to condemn to extermination by exploitation or indifference any animal or plant which was of no direct benefit to us for food or pleasure.

I am firmly of the opinion that it is practically possible to meet the legitimate needs of the human population without destroying the chances of the remaining wild populations. However, if we are to achieve that it will need sympathy, restraint, understanding and very careful planning by governments, industries and conservationists.

from the fourth Jane Hodge Memorial Lecture, The Institute of
Science and Technology
CARDIFF, 23 NOVEMBER 1973

What You Can Do for the Cause of Conservation

At this conference* we have all heard a lot of facts and analyses about our situation on space-ship earth. We have been reminded that there is an interdependence of man and nature and that man has acquired an immense power over his environment.

This means that man must accept responsibilities in proportion to his power and, if we are to exercise these responsibilities so that all life can continue on earth, they must have a moral and philosophical basis. Simple self-interest, economic profit and absolute materialism are no longer enough.

It has been made perfectly clear that a concern for any part of life on this planet – human, plant or animal, wild or tame – is a concern for all life. A threat to any part of the environment is a threat to the whole environment, but we must have a basis of assessment of these threats, not so that we can establish a priority of fears, but so that we can make a positive contribution to improvement and ultimate survival.

I think we are all convinced of the righteousness of our cause. This is splendid, but I must sound a note of warning: we are still a long way from convincing all the other people who need to be convinced. We must not delude ourselves. For one thing, we must realise that there is a very large body of opinion which not only considers wild animals a bore, but also considers that anyone wet enough to be interested in them is a crank and a crackpot. This doesn't make it any easier to get the message through.

* The World Wildlife Fund Congress, London, 1970.

It is unlikely that this body will ever be convinced and I dare say they will happily die from the effects of pollution before admitting anything is wrong. We must realise that they will certainly not be convinced by excessive fastidiousness or unreasonable extremism in any form.

Prophets of doom are never welcome anyway, so we must be very careful about the arguments we use and the issues we choose. We must be very careful to avoid plugging our pet hates unless we are quite sure that they really are significant in the total picture. Selecting a doubtful issue is counter-productive and merely gives comfort to the cynics and to those who simply don't want to know about anything which might disturb their self-satisfaction.

We will get nowhere if we start making demands which are obviously unacceptable to the majority. You cannot convert a materialistic society overnight; you can only hope to modify its worst excesses. You cannot defeat self-interest in one easy lesson; it takes time, persistence and a patient and intelligent teacher.

It is, of course, quite natural to do the obvious thing first. We look around to see who the decision-makers are and the obvious thing is to give them our valuable advice and then to assume that the rest will follow. We can tell industry what it should do and shipowners or aircraft manufacturers what they should do. There are even quite a lot of us ready and willing to tell governments and the United Nations exactly what they should do about it. The trouble is that they won't take this advice until they have understood the problem.

We can also ride our particular hobby horse. Some want this banned and that prevented, others want anything from more national parks and nature reserves to controls on economic development and a restriction on the exploitation of natural resources: legislation against greed and laws against gadgets.

The message of conservation may, indeed it must, be logical, sensible and morally sound, but nothing will happen unless we can mobilise public opinion. As public opinion is nothing more than an identity of view between a large number of individual people, the answer is that we must get the conservation message through to as many people as possible.

The very first thing we must do is to be sure that we are giving the right message, that we have got the facts and the arguments right without bias, prejudice or special pleading.

Therefore, I suggest the very first thing to do is to learn more about the subject and to discover more about the factors involved. Learn about natural history, read about pollution, think about the population statistics, enquire about the world's renewable and non-renewable resources. In fact, make a real effort to understand the situation this planet earth finds itself in at this present time and what is likely to happen in the future. Consider the implications and worry about the moral justification for conservation.

After that you have got to go out and talk to your friends and bore your acquaintances. You have got to allow your concern for conservation to influence your decisions and practice at all times. It is no good going to a meeting like this, voting piously for a resolution and then going back to the office and forgetting all about it. It is no use complaining about oil on the beaches and then leaving all your rubbish about next time you have a picnic.

The best form of communication and persuasion is by precept and example. A good example in your treatment of the environment will be noticed and copied, particularly by children.

If you feel strongly about conservation, let that concern influence your decisions at whatever work you may be doing. Make sure that conservation factors are raised and discussed in relation to current operations and new developments in business, local or central government.

Write letters. Write to the papers or to your Member of Parliament, to ministers, political as well as ecclesiastical, and indeed to anyone in the public eye. I get a lot of letters of this sort and, apart from being interesting and helpful to me, although some perhaps not quite as rational as others, it is surprising how much can be achieved by putting the right people in touch with each other.

It is not always necessary to write to people giving your views and opinions. It is frequently more rewarding merely to ask pertinent questions. It may get someone to go and look for an answer. If you get a silly answer, which can easily happen, you can return to the charge with even more telling effect. Whatever happens, don't give up and don't despair. Results may not be immediately apparent, but you may have touched a receptive chord without knowing it. Even the most unsympathetic and un-enlightened politician, industrialist or bureaucrat begins to take notice when a lot of people write about the same subject.

If you can appear on television or in films or if you can gather an audience for a lecture, these are obviously valuable contribu-tions. However, don't forget that audiences are also needed, so if you can't talk, listen: support lectures and discussion groups.

There is, of course, a limit to what people can do on their own, so I suggest that if you have not done so already, join and get your friends to join a local, national or international society or organisation concerned with some aspect of conservation. This could be anything from societies concerned with the protection of particular animals or plants to naturalists' societies or associa-tions concerned with conservation as a whole. If you can't find one that suits your interests, get together with your friends and form a new society.

I have put forward these not very original suggestions for personal action because one thing is absolutely certain. Unless a great and growing number of people are prepared to keep up the pressure, individually as well as collectively, nothing will happen. Perhaps to be more accurate I should say that the wrong things will happen and we shall damage this planet beyond any hope of repair or recovery.

There is ample evidence around us of the way people can dedicate themselves to destruction. How much more rewarding to dedicate yourself to conservation. There may be this specialist view and that vested interest, but in the end we all have a vested interest in the future survival of this earth and the happiness of our children and grandchildren who will find themselves living on it.

It is an old cliché to say that the future is in the hands of the young. This is no longer true. The quality of life to be enjoyed or the existence to be survived by our children and future generations is in our hands now.

Closing Address to the World Wildlife Fund Congress
LONDON, 18 NOVEMBER 1970

Index of Names

(including organisations addressed)